RECOLLECTIONS OF
LIFE ON THE
PRISON SHIP
Jersey

RECOLLECTIONS OF
LIFE ON THE
PRISON SHIP
Jersey

in 1782

THOMAS DRING

A Revolutionary War-Era Manuscript

Edited by David Swain

WESTHOLME
Yardley

Frontispiece: "Interior of the old Jersey prison ship in the Revolutionary War," by Felix O. C. Darley, engraved by Edward Bookhout, 1855. (*Library of Congress*)

First Paperback Edition 2019
Introduction, notes, and transcription © 2010 David Swain
Map by Tracy Dungan © 2010 Westholme Publishing

Westholme Publishing, LLC
904 Edgewood Road
Yardley, Pennsylvania 19067
Visit our Web site at www.westholmepublishing.com

ISBN: 978-1-59416-335-7
Also available as an eBook.

Printed in the United States of America.

To those who have sacrificed in war
And those who work toward peace

CONTENTS

EDITOR'S INTRODUCTION

During the first half of the nineteenth century, human bones regularly washed up on the mud banks of Wallabout Bay, along the Brooklyn shore of the East River, opposite Manhattan, New York City. Dredging in the mud flats for construction of the Brooklyn Navy Yard (begun in 1801 and expanded periodically for a century or more) exposed many more human remains. History tells us that these are the bones of perhaps as many as twelve thousand American men who fought in the Revolutionary War and were captured and imprisoned on the infamous British prison ship *Jersey*. They died on board the hulk, and were hastily interred by fellow prisoners in the nearby mud banks.

The bones of those who died tell mutely their own dismal tale. A survivor of *Jersey* imprisonment in 1782 named Thomas Dring has left us his own tale, written out in a lengthy, detailed, and impassioned manuscript narrative of his personal experiences and their aftermath. Written in 1824, late in his life and forty years after his prison ship ordeal, Dring's narrative presents one man's recollections of the inhumanities of war inflicted during America's Revolutionary War. His describes his prison ship ordeal as an experience partly of intentionally cruel atrocities committed by man against man, partly of human neglect and callous indifference in the face of extreme suffering, and partly of the ravages of filth and uncontrollable disease upon closely confined prisoners.

Thomas Dring was born at Newport, Rhode Island, on August 3, 1758. A seaman by trade, he chose privateering as his contribution to America's revolutionary cause. During the age of sailing ships, privateering was a commonly accepted and officially adopted method of economic warfare designed to disrupt the movement of supplies and materiel to enemy military forces and the flow of commerce to and from enemy territory. (The invention of the submarine later transformed this method of warfare into a covert and calculated hunt for commercial shipping on the high seas, beginning in World War I.) By authorizing private ships to engage in privateer operations, a warring government could augment its naval force and free its warships for direct combat with the enemy's navy. By arming their ships and sailing to capture enemy ships (called prizes) and their cargoes, those engaged in privateering played a high-stakes game of chance that could be extremely lucrative—or could result in capture of the privateer ship and imprisonment of the crew by the enemy. In practice, little separated privateering from piracy, except that it was deemed "legal" by the authorizing government.

During the Revolutionary War, the Continental Congress authorized privateering on March 19, 1776. Privateer ships were made "legal" by being licensed with an official "letter of marque and reprisal." Responding to the potential opportunity for quick though risky profit, many who during peacetime were engaged in commercial trade and shipping—ship owners, captains, officers, and ordinary seamen—soon turned privateering into a popular contribution to the war effort, especially in the New England states. Their effectiveness soon became evident. A February 1778 report to the British House of Commons calculated that American privateers had already taken 733 prizes. During the same year, American sources reported a total of 115 privateer ships in operation. By 1781 that number had quadrupled to 449.[1]

1. See Richard B. Morris, *Encyclopedia of American History*, rev. ed. (New York: Harper and Row, 1961), 89, 99.

Bad luck first overtook Dring when his privateer ship was captured by the British in about June 1779, resulting in his first prison ship experience, on the *Good Hope*. This prison ship (a former navy ship with thirty-four guns) had a capacity, once stripped of guns, etc., of about five hundred prisoners. Located in the North (Hudson) River when Dring was imprisoned on it, the *Good Hope* was moved to Wallabout Bay along the East River in January 1780, and burned there three months later. After apparently four or five months of captivity, he dramatically escaped in October with ten companions.[2] Following this escape, he returned to privateering. In May 1780, he sailed from Providence, Rhode Island aboard the privateer *General Washington*, owned by John Brown, and successfully completed a privateering venture.[3] Not until May 1782 (when Dring was twenty-three years old) did his luck turn bad again. This time he sailed from Providence on the privateer *Chance*, which was quickly captured by the British. He and his fellow crewmen were incarcerated on the prison ship *Jersey* at Wallabout Bay, remaining there for two months, after which those remaining alive and well were exchanged. After the war ended, Dring returned to the sea as a merchant seaman, soon becoming captain of a vessel. But he retired from the sea in 1803 and established himself in business in Providence, where he resided until his death on August 8, 1825. Only late in his life, at age sixty-five, did Dring decide to write a narrative describing his experiences while a prisoner on the *Jersey*.

2. This escape is described in the *Trenton New-Jersey Gazette*, October 12, 1779, as having occurred the previous Wednesday at one o'clock in the morning. Quoted in Henry Onderdonk Jr., *Revolutionary Incidents of Suffolk and Kings Counties*. . . . (New York: Leavitt, 1849), 230.

3. See unpublished manuscripts of William Drowne (who later on was himself a *Jersey* prisoner) printed in Henry B. Dawson's editorial appendix to Thomas Dring and Albert G. Greene, *Recollections of the Jersey Prison-Ship* (Morrisania, NY, 1865), 166 (see note 9).

Despite their horrible conditions, the ships the British used as floating prisons during the Revolutionary War reflected several centuries of military reform toward more humane treatment of captured combatants. Since the advent of human warfare, the common practice had been to slaughter or enslave captured combatants.[4] In Europe, as the Middle Ages ended, more humanistic values of the Renaissance and later the Enlightenment emerged and blossomed. These values spawned a new, more humane concept that wartime incarceration was preferable to the age-old practices of massacre or slavery.

Unlike slavery or death, imprisonment was not supposed to be a terminal condition. It was expected to last only as long as the military conflict continued, after which (or perhaps before) prisoners could expect to be released, as dictated by terms of a joint prisoner exchange, repatriation, or peace treaty. With this new concept in play, depending on the war situation, prison conditions, and prisoner treatment, combatants might now conclude that incarceration was preferable to continuing to fight.

Historically, the major European powers first formally agreed in the 1648 Treaty of Westphalia that ended the Thirty

4. The so-called barbaric practices of massacre and slavery in ancient warfare are well documented. See, for instance, Christian S. Archer, John P. Ferris, Holger H. Herwig, and Timothy H. E. Travers, *World History of Warfare* (Lincoln: University of Nebraska Press, 2002). They cite examples such as: capture of prisoners for mass religious sacrifices in Shang China (eleventh century BCE) (49); Greek slaughter of non-Hellenic and later Hellenic enemy combatants captured in battle (fifth century BCE) (72); and usually enslavement but sometimes freedom or execution of those captured by Alexander the Great's army (fourth century BCE). They also document similar war practices in much more recent times, for example, mutual atrocities by British and Indians during the so-called Indian Mutiny in 1857 (468); regular massacres by Spanish soldiers of South American independence fighters in the early nineteenth century (453); and mutual genocide by German and Russian troops (more methodical and widespread by the Germans) during World War II (520).

Years War that prisoners of war should be treated humanely and released at the end of hostilities. These general concepts were gradually elaborated and codified into a body of international law defining the status, rights, acceptable treatment, and potential means for release of prisoners of war. Under these rules, the basic human rights of prisoners were supposed to be preserved by enforcing what was generally accepted at the time as "humane" methods of treatment. In practice, as with much else in warfare, the standards of humanity were often honored in the breach. These rules, as they had evolved between the 1650s and 1770s, were applied by both the Americans and British during the Revolutionary War. By this time, the rules were pretty much taken for granted as accepted policies among the rules of war—but their enforcement in practice was frequently the subject of complaints and controversy.[5]

During the Revolutionary War, inhumane conditions and treatment of prisoners made the experience of wartime incarceration one of physical hardship, emotional stress, and psychological humiliation. The accumulated miseries—rotted and/or infested food (and little of that), polluted water, cramped and unsanitary conditions—caused the death of large numbers of prisoners during their confinement. In this case, therefore, and in many others, recent and less recent, the humanitarian hopes for imprisonment over death or slavery were not fulfilled in practice.

Incarcerating thousands of enemy combatants during a major military conflict requires the availability of large numbers of large prisons. During the Revolutionary War, the British were at a disadvantage in this regard because they reliably controlled relatively little territory and few large buildings. They did control New York City for some time, and they turned sev-

5. For a general summary about prisoners of war in the rules of warfare and international law, see *Encyclopedia Britannica*, s.v. "Prisoner of War."

eral buildings there into prisons, especially Van Cortlandt's Sugar House and the city's New Jail, which was turned into a "provost" prison for officers. A couple of churches also were converted into prisons, including North Dutch Church, which, with its pews removed, temporarily housed eight hundred prisoners in 1776. Because these land prisons became totally inadequate to accommodate the large numbers of prisoners the British were accumulating through military victories and ship captures, they devised a new solution–the creation of floating prisons using "used up" British navy ships. Some of these were anchored in the North (Hudson) and East Rivers as early as 1776. Soon they were concentrated in the shallow channels, among the mud flats of Wallabout Bay, in the East River next to the Brooklyn shore across from lower Manhattan Island.[6]

A number of ships served as British prisons or as floating hospitals at Wallabout Bay, but never more than about five at a time. The *Jersey* was the largest and most notorious of these.

6. While the British navy occupied Newport, Rhode Island, between 1776 and 1779, prison ships were used here as well to incarcerate captives, mostly New England privateer seamen. According to Christian M. McBurney, "British Treatment of Prisoners During the Occupation of Newport, 1776–1779: Disease, Starvation and Death Stalk the Prison Ships," *Newport History* 79 (2010), the prison ship experience of American captives at Newport was, generally speaking, somewhat less lethal, and conditions were somewhat better, than in New York, except during a period in 1778 when both starvation and illness took their toll. By the time the British evacuated Newport, they had released most of their prisoners. They transferred the remaining few to prison ships in New York. Meanwhile, the British also were finding other, domestic uses for prison ships. After the American Revolution deprived them of their most useful destination for "transported convicts," they turned to Australia, recently "discovered" by Captain James Cook. During the 1780s and 1790s, old naval hulks were anchored in the Thames River at Woolwich, downstream from London. These were used as temporary prisons for convicts brought from local jails, while they awaited ships to carry them to Australia. Of course, the conditions on these prison ships were abominable, as they were also on the transport ships. See sources such as

She had been a 60-gun, 1,000-ton fourth rate ship-of-the-line with a crew of 450, built in 1736. After arriving at the Wallabout, she was permanently anchored, and her guns, sails, rigging, and masts were all removed. With a capacity of one thousand prisoners or more (as the British figured it), she served as the "receiving" ship for all prisoners not initially "ill." Those deemed ill were sent directly to a nearby hospital ship.[7]

In 1782, Dring spent his entire imprisonment time on the *Jersey*. His only comparative frame of reference was the *Good Hope* in 1779, which he found more humane—and from which he escaped. His fascinating and graphic descriptions of the horrible conditions he experienced aboard the *Jersey* make up the bulk of his manuscript. Clearly, his memory of these conditions impelled him, late in life, to put pen to paper to recollect his own agonies so that his fellow countrymen, a quarter of the way through the nineteenth century, would remember with him, and be appalled at the experience and awed at the sacrifice.

Even as he sought, long after the conflict, to kindle the flame of reverence for the memory of those who had suffered and died, Dring expresses in his narrative righteous indignation against the great majority of his fellow countrymen who, at the time, neglected the American inmates on the prison ships. He is distressed that they did not flock forward with donations of money, food, and clothing, nor is he happy about the

Charles F. Campbell, *The Intolerable Hulks: British Shipboard Confinement, 1776–1857* (Tucson, AZ: Fenestar Books, 2001), and Thomas Keneally, *A Commonwealth of Thieves* (Milsons Point, NSW, Australia: Random House, 2005), or, for a graphic fictional description, see Colleen McCullough, *Morgan's Run* (New York: Simon and Schuster, 2000).

7. See Eugene L. Armbruster, *The Wallabout Prison Ships, 1776–1783* (New York: privately printed, 1920), copy in the University of California Library, available via Internet Archive, http://www.archive.org/stream/wallabout-prison00armbrich/wallaboutprison00armbrich_djvu.txt.

American "central" government's (Continental Congress, after 1781 under the Articles of Confederation) failure to arrange prompt exchanges.

Thomas Dring's manuscript, now in the possession of the Rhode Island Historical Society, covers seventy-nine closely and neatly written pages. Although he certainly desired that it be read by others, he apparently had no specific intentions of having it published. After his death, however, Albert G. Greene (subsequently director of the RIHS) did publish it in 1829, though only after he had performed some drastic editorial surgery, leaving the narrative largely unrecognizable in comparison with the original. To his credit, however, this surgery destroyed neither Dring's attitudes nor his story, except for his appendix, which Greene ignored, perhaps because he knew that much of it was copied from another book.[8] Greene himself acknowledged in his preface the scope of his rewriting, asserting that it was necessary in order to create a readable and organized narrative out of what he considered to be Dring's disorganized manuscript. Greene nowhere reveals the fact that Dring copied passages without attribution from an early work written for the Tammany Society, *An Account of the Interment of the Remains of 11,500 American Seamen. . .* (1808); possibly he did not know of it himself, although this seems unlikely. The Dring–Greene narrative proved sufficiently popular to be reprinted several times, in 1831, 1865, and 1961.[9] No one until now, however, has gone back to the original manuscript. It is published here for the first time.

8. See pages xxxiv and 121.

9. The original 1829 volume was published by H. H. Brown in Providence under the title *Recollections of the Jersey Prison-Ship*, which title was maintained on later editions. In 1831, P. M. Davis of New York published an almost identical edition with only the pagination changed. The 1865 edition reprinted exactly the 1831 version, but in addition, Henry B. Dawson, then of Morrisania, New York, who both published and edited this volume, inserted

Dring's style is emotional, and he leaves no doubt about his feelings concerning what he experienced on the *Jersey*.[10] He sees himself as a patriotic hero who endured–for the sacred cause of freedom–great misery, deprivation, and almost death, which he feels compelled to tell in detail for the benefit of posterity. Beyond that, he sees himself as a particularly clever, as well as lucky, hero who managed in various ways to subvert the death-dealing system by such precautions as inoculating himself against smallpox, not eating meat cooked in the common "copper," and not attempting to escape. As a fervent patriot, he expounds upon the fortitude of the prisoners, who, he claims, virtually always preferred death in the *Jersey* to joining the British service in order to obtain relief from their suffering. He does not consider escape to be a viable third alternative. Bitter antipathy toward the tyrannical British enemy is the other side of Dring's patriotic coin. But Dring's most withering distain is reserved for the refugees or loyalists, who, he recalls, did worse than just follow orders; they enjoyed being cruel. Interestingly enough, the Hessian mercenaries are considered

---

a lengthy introduction, extensive footnotes, and a bulky appendix quoting numerous relevant documents. His introduction is especially interesting because of the pro-British view he takes concerning the rights and treatment of prisoners in the American rebellion of 1775, probably reflecting a pro-Northern attitude toward the Southern rebellion of 1861, as well as his somewhat revisionist approach to history (see David D. Van Tassel, "Henry Barton Dawson: A Nineteenth-Century Revisionist," *William and Mary Quarterly,* 3rd ser., 13 (1956): 319–41). The 1961 edition, published by Corinth Books in New York, is a photocopy of the 1829 edition with a short introduction by Professor Lawrence H. Leder of Brandeis University. See note 4 to Dring's narrative for an explanation of the copied sources.

10. Some of the more emotional language, however, is not Dring's but was copied from the 1808 book produced by the Tammany Society, *An Account of the Interment of the Remains of 11,500 American Seamen;* see note 4 to Dring's narrative. Still, Dring clearly espouses the feelings expressed in the material he copied and reiterates them in his own words elsewhere in the narrative.

XVIII   EDITOR'S INTRODUCTION

the only relatively compassionate prison guards on the *Jersey*, possibly because they had no particular emotional stake in the contest.

Scattered throughout his narrative, Dring does allow other, more positive, facets of human nature to shine through his dominant memories of cruelty, callousness, and disease. Simple human enjoyments such as successfully securing firewood and smoking a pipe become remarkable events. Even certain evidences of human caring and kindness among the prisoners (especially himself) are acknowledged. In short, besides being an interesting and arresting historical document, Dring's narrative is a revealing and sobering reflection upon the human condition.

As a ship's officer in a society of gentlemen, Dring makes it clear that he expected, even from his captors, better than bare subsistence treatment. Gentlemen expected a bit of extra comfort, a bit of special recognition of rank. But since the British chose on the *Jersey* to treat all prisoners (at least all American prisoners) equally, Dring and the other captive officers were reduced to creating their own class society between decks, ironically including equality of treatment in their definition of British tyranny.

A reading of Dring's narrative raises several key issues. The first concerns whether his views are close to the reality of conditions on the *Jersey*. A man who was captive on the *Jersey* in 1779 gives a relatively positive account of conditions then.[11] This is about the same time that Dring was a prisoner on the *Good Hope*, about which his recollections are also fairly positive. But conditions did get worse—and then somewhat better. They depended to some extent, apparently, on how much effort and care the British officer currently in charge expended

11. Daniel Stanton was on the *Jersey* for three or four weeks, after which he was transferred to the *Good Hope*. See the *New London Connecticut Gazette*, September 1, 1779, printed in the Papers of the New London Historical Society, vol. 4, 44.

in overseeing the prison ship operations. Vice-Admiral John Byron, who replaced Vice-Admiral Richard Howe in 1779, made a conscious effort to improve conditions, apparently with some success. In December 1780 he was replaced, however, by Admiral George Brydges Rodney, who quickly gained a reputation for cruelty. Not until 1782, when General Guy Carleton replaced Lieutenant General Henry Clinton as overall British commander in America (with Rear Admiral Robert Digby under him), were conditions consciously improved again. Although this change coincided with the *Jersey* prisoners' petition to General Washington described by Dring, the petition and its results were probably more symptoms than causes of Carleton's new policy.[12]

Conditions could never be called good, however. The *Jersey* justifiably gained an evil reputation, which is reflected in virtually every contemporary newspaper account, prison letter, and published narrative, of which quite a number are extant.[13]

12. General Carleton had orders to "wind down" the war and conciliate the Americans while awaiting a formal peace treaty. See Edgar Stanton McClay, *History of American Privateers* (New York: Appleton, 1899), 148 (from the account of prisoner Joshua Barney); and Gardner W. Allen, *Naval History of the American Revolution* (Boston: Houghton Mifflin, 1913), 2:638.

13. The major narratives include H. Caritat, ed., *An Historical Sketch . . . of the Life of Silas Talbot. . . .* (New York: G. and R. Waite, 1803) (hereafter cited as *Silas Talbot*); *Memoirs of Andrew Sherburne. . . .* (Providence, RI: H. H. Brown, 1831); Charles I. Bushnell, ed., *The Adventures of Christopher Hawkins. . . .* (New York: privately printed, 1864); Thomas Andros, *The Old Jersey Captive. . . .* (Boston: William Pierce, 1833), reprinted in the *Magazine of History* (1916), extra no. 46; *The Adventures of Ebenezer Fox. . . .* (Boston: Charles Fox, 1838); Philip Freneau, "The British Prison Ship", written in 1780, in *The Poems of Philip Freneau. . . .* 1839, Fred Lewis Pattee Collection on The Poems of Philip Freneau, 1900–1905, vol. 2, Manuscripts Division, Princeton University Library; Alexander Coffin Jr. to U.S. Representative Dr. Samuel L. Mitchell, 4 September 1807, printed in Dawson's appendix, Dring-Greene, *Recollections*, 181–88; Alexander Coffin Jr., *Interment of the Martyrs* (Brooklyn, [186?]), quoted from in Bushnell's notes to *Adventures of Christopher Hawkins*, 233–36, 271–72; John Van Dyke's unpublished narrative printed in Bushnell's notes to *Adventures of Christopher Hawkins*, 215–17.

Although these various accounts support Dring's narrative in many instances, they tend to bring into question his assertion that successful escape from the *Jersey* was practically impossible. Even his own evidence shows that, although a tricky business requiring a good deal of luck, successful escapes did occur from time to time. Other narratives also show that many more prisoners than Dring admits to enlisted in the British service to relieve their sufferings on the *Jersey* (while others were impressed). A few at least enlisted with the perfectly patriotic notion that escaping from the British service would be easier than from the *Jersey*. One such enlistee, Ebenezer Fox, was transferred to Kingston, Jamaica, before he was able to escape to Cuba, finally returning home with the French fleet.[14]

A second important issue concerns how conditions on the *Jersey* compared with those both in other British prisons and in American prisons. Concerning conditions in general in other British prisons at New York and in England, soldiers fared better than sailors, naval personnel better than privateersmen, those in land prisons better than those in prison ships, officers better than enlistees (the higher the rank, the better the treatment), and those in England better than those in America. It seems that because the privateersmen were considered by the British to be rebel pirates rather than prisoners of war, and because there were no arrangements for official exchanges of privateersmen, these unwanted and unfortunate prisoners were relegated to the prison ships, the worst and most crowded prisons the British operated in North America.[15] Land prisons at New York, especially the Provost (a VIP prison) and the Sugar

14. Fox's description of life on the *Jersey* is occasionally strangely similar to the Dring-Greene account published just a few years before. There can be little doubt, however, of the unique authenticity of the description of his enlistment and escape. See *Adventures of Ebenezer Fox*, 147.

15 In "British Treatment of Prisoners," Christian M. McBurney offers a more differentiated interpretation, pointing out that, compared with the prison ship experience of American captives in New York, imprisonment in Newport

House, about which there were copious complaints, were nevertheless not as malignant as the prison ships.[16] No privateersmen were sent to these prisons, however, except for an occasional captain. Other privateer captains (as well as other high-ranking officers), among them Captain Daniel Aborn of the *Chance*, were paroled to live with loyalist families on Long Island or even to return home, but their crews were sent to the prison ships.[17] Among the various prison ships, conditions were apparently not that different, except perhaps in those used exclusively as hospital ships, as Dring suggests. The cause of the *Jersey's* especially notorious reputation was its primary use as a receiving ship for arriving prisoners. All prisoners entered here; not all left again.[18]

prison ships was statistically less lethal, and conditions were demonstrably better, especially after a grim period during 1778.

16. Major sources on life in other New York prisons include Caritat, *Silas Talbot*, 126–28; John Fell's diary (1777–1778) printed in Onderdonk, *Revolutionary Incidents*, 219–26; Jonathan Gillett to Eliza Gillett, 2 December 1776, in Danske Dandridge, *American Prisoners of the Revolution* (1911; repr., Baltimore: Genealogical Publishing, 1967), 28–31; *Journal of Elias Cornelius . . . 1777 and 1778. . . .* (Washington, DC: Charles M. Tompkins and Chester T. Sherman, 1903); David L. Sterling, ed., "American Prisoners of War in New York: A Report by Elias Boudinot," *William and Mary Quarterly*, 3rd ser., 13 (1956): 376–93. There is further material of interest in Onderdonk, *Revolutionary Incidents,* 207–18, 226–27, 245–49; Dandridge, *American Prisoners,* 33–111, 123–51.

17. For a description of the parole system for high-ranking officers, see Charles Patrick Neimeyer, *The Revolutionary War* (Westport, CT: Greenwood Press, 2007), 73–74.

18. The best descriptions we have of hospital ship conditions are in the *Memoirs of Andrew Sherburne*, 113–16, and in Freneau, *Poems*, 32–39. For descriptions of life on other prison ships see Robert Sheffield's letter in the *New London Connecticut Gazette*, July 10, 1778, printed in Onderdonk, *Revolutionary Incidents,* 227–28, and a letter from a prisoner on the *Falmouth* also in the *Connecticut Gazette*, May 25, 1780 (ibid., 231). See also Onderdonk, *Revolutionary Incidents,* 227–41, and Bushnell's notes in *Adventures of Christopher Hawkins*, 238–41.

The American privateer prisoners of all ranks in the Old Mill and Forton prisons at Plymouth and Portsmouth, England, respectively, lived a much more humane existence. Better conditions make for higher expectations, however, and the prisoners listed many complaints in their diaries and in petitions. Repeated attempts to escape from these prisons and a fair number of enlistments in the British service also reveal the depth of prisoner discontent.[19]

The Americans also maintained prisons both on land and in ships. The evidence suggests that the Americans were not, in

19. For further details on this subject see note 44 to Dring's narrative and the references to other notes listed therein. Major sources on life in Old Mill and Forton prisons include *Silas Talbot; Memoirs of Andrew Sherburne*; Charles Herbert, *A Relic of the Revolution*, ed. Richard Livesey (Boston: Charles M. Pierce, 1847); *The Memoirs of Nathaniel Fanning*. . . . (New York, 1806), reprinted in the *Magazine of History*, extra no. 21, 1913; "Diary of William Widger . . . 1781," *Essex Institute Historical Collections* 73 (1937): 311–347; 74 (1938): 22–48, 142–158; Marion S. Coan, ed., "A Revolutionary Prison Diary, 1777–1779: The Journal of Dr. Jonathan Haskins," *New England Quarterly* 16 (1944): 290–309; 17 (1944): 424–42; "A Yankee Privateersman [Timothy Connor] in Prison in England, [diary] 1777–1779," *New England Historical and Genealogical Register* 30 (1876): 175–77, 343–52; 31 (1877): 18–20, 212–13, 284–88; 32 (1878): 70–73, 165–68, 280–86; "Prison Ships and the 'Old Mill Prison,' Plymouth, England, 1777" (extracts of Samuel Cutler's diary), *New England Historical and Genealogical Register* 32 (1878): 42–44, 184–88, 305–8, 395–98. An interesting article by John K. Alexander, ("Jonathan Haskins' Mill Prison 'Diary': Can it be Accepted at Face Value?" *New England Quarterly* 40 (1967): 561–64) explores the probability that Haskins borrowed some sections of his diary from Charles Herbert's diary, and that Samuel Cutler's diary might have been involved also. He concludes, however, that whatever plagiarism may have taken place, the basic accuracy of the three diaries "cannot be dismissed." See also the chapter on Joshua Barney, in McClay, *History of American Privateers*, 148–66, and Allen, *Naval History*, 638–58. Benjamin Franklin's activities in England concerning both privateering and exchange of American prisoners are interestingly described in William Bell Clark's *Benjamin Franklin's Privateers: A Naval Epic of the American Revolution* (Baton Rouge: Louisiana State University Press, 1956).

general, any more humane captors than their enemies. British military officials complained regularly to the Americans about bad treatment of prisoners incarcerated at Philadelphia, in a mine in Connecticut, and on prison ships at Esopus Landing, New York, Boston, Massachusetts, and the Connecticut towns of Stonington and New London; at the latter in 1782, the Americans established a prison ship christened the *Retaliation*.[20] It does not appear that American prison ships were more luxurious dungeons than the British variety, except that perhaps the American ships could more easily and wholesomely be supplied with provisions from the hinterland.

The so-called Convention Army provides an anomalous and interesting example of American prisoner-of-war practices at perhaps their worst. In the fall of 1777, following British Lieutenant General John Burgoyne's surrender of his thirty-two-hundred-man army after losing the Battle of Saratoga, he signed a "convention" with American Major General Horatio

20. Edward Floyd DeLancey, editor of loyalist Thomas Jones's *History of New York during the Revolutionary War.* . . . (written in England shortly after the war, published by the New York Historical Society in 1879) has supplied a valuable footnote containing information on American use of the Ulster County, New York, prison and prison ships at Esopus Landing early in the war (1:705–9). See also Allen, *Naval History,* 655. Examples of British complaints about American prison conditions include a letter by Admiral Marriot Arbuthnot to General Washington, April 21, 1781, complaining especially of the lack of fuel and a diet of salted clams at the Philadelphia prison, printed in Dawson's appendix, Dring-Greene, *Recollections,* 130; David Sproat to Abraham Skinner, American commissary of prisoners, June 30, 1782, printed in Dawson's appendix, 151–53. In *Forgotten Patriots: American Prisoners of War in the Revolutionary War* (New York: Basic Books, 2008), 189, Edwin G. Burrows concludes that the harsh conditions in these prison ships were not far different from those in British prison ships such as the *Jersey*. Esopus Landing was located well up the Hudson River from New York City, where Rondout Creek flows into the river near Kingston, in Ulster County. Three prison ships, soon collectively dubbed the Fleet Prison, were in use there in 1782.

Gates concerning the fate of the prisoner army. The convention itself was unusual and caused difficulties, partly because it declared the army not to be prisoners of war (they were treated as such anyway), and Congress rescinded it in 1778.

Meanwhile, lacking facilities for that many prisoners of war, the Americans essentially marched the men around until the end of the war. First they were marched to Massachusetts, where they camped for a year. Later, they were marched to Virginia, then back northward to Maryland, later to Pennsylvania, until finally back to Massachusetts. As described by Edwin Burrows in *Forgotten Patriots*, "Almost every step of the way they contended with meager rations, shortages of fuel, inadequate accommodations, and physical violence"–the latter because of hostility among local residents.[21] In this case the problem was not an overcrowded prison or intentionally cruel treatment by guards. In fact, the American guards may have been about as bad off as the British prisoners. This was simply a case of neglect and indecision. Interestingly, disease and mortality appear to have been not so severe a threat among this army as they were on the prison ships.

A third relevant issue concerns whether complaints of conditions on the *Jersey* are justifiable in terms of then-recognized legalities of war as well as the laws of humanity. It seems clear that Dring's list of woes demonstrates serious violations of the laws of humanity, even though his viewpoint is that of an officer-gentleman used to the extra niceties of life. According to the laws of England, however, the privateer prisoners were not prisoners of war. Instead they were traitors, pirates, and rebels against His Britannic Majesty.[22] To at least some of the British and loyalist men entrusted with the "care" of American priva-

21. Burrows, *Forgotten Patriots*, 188.

22. The best source on this subject is Worthington Chauncey Ford's editorial notes in *Correspondence and Journals of Samuel Blackley Webb*, 3 vols. (New York: Wickersham, 1893–94), especially vol. 2, 19–85 (hereafter cited as

teersmen prisoners, this legal assessment provided an easy excuse for contemptuous neglect or active cruelty, both of which seem to have been practiced. Naturally the Americans rejected the British version of their legal status, and desired to be recognized as and treated with the full rights of prisoners of war. Although they felt their claim to be legitimate, they were not in a position to influence their own status, and by its inaction on the subject, their central government ratified the British definition of their status.

During the American Civil War, the nearest equivalent to privateering were the attempts to run the Union blockade of Southern seaports, but this yielded few prisoners of war. However, a different, more significant situation during that war somewhat paralleled the irregular status of Revolutionary War privateersmen as prisoners of war. In the Civil War, after the Emancipation Proclamation, the "irregular" prisoners of war were African Americans serving in the Union army. Officially, General Robert E. Lee and the Confederacy held to the doctrine that African American prisoners were not persons with

Samuel Blackley Webb). General Gage first declared Americans in arms to be "rebels and traitors" on June 12, 1775, a position which was upheld by royal decree on August 23. On August 13, Gage had written to General Washington that American prisoners would be "treated with care and kindness . . . indiscriminately, it is true, for I acknowledge no rank that is not derived from the king" (Ford's note, *Samuel Blackley Webb*, 2: 19–20). On February 6, 1777, Lord North guided through Parliament a bill allowing British forces to capture and imprison American privateersmen, defining their status as pirates and traitors but removing their rights as accused criminals of habeas corpus and a speedy trial (see British *Annual Register* 20:53, quoted in George T. Curtis, "Report on Exchange of Prisoners During the American Revolution," December 19, 1861, in the *Proceedings of the Massachusetts Historical Society* 1861: 329). In the spring of 1782 Parliament, finally recognizing that Britain was losing the war, agreed to drop treason charges against all these American prisoners, none of whom had ever been tried, and to change their status to prisoner of war in order to facilitate exchange or release (see Allen, *Naval History,* 657).

rights, but escaped slave property that (who) should be returned to their masters. Lieutenant General Ulysses S. Grant and the Union countered that all captured combatants were human beings and deserved equal treatment. When some African American prisoners did indeed arrive at the Andersonville prison camp in 1864, the commandant there had to make a decision about how to treat them. After requesting orders and, as he recalled later, receiving a response of "until further orders treat them as prisoners of war," he did what practicality necessitated anyway–treated all his thousands of prisoners alike.[23]

Additional interesting comparisons can potentially be made with prisoner-of-war practices during the American Civil War. Neither side operated prison ships of the kind used in the Revolutionary War, but both operated large land prisons. By far the most notorious of these, both because of its inhumane conditions and because the Union victors were able to make an example of it, was the Confederate prison camp at Andersonville, Georgia.

This huge prison was built in late 1863 and early 1864 to relieve pressure on a number of prisons in Virginia, and to free up Confederate soldiers farther north for combat duty. Guard duty at Andersonville was assigned to Georgia militia deemed not fit for combat. The prison was designed for 10,000 prisoners. However, when military urgency led to its premature opening in February 1864, a wooden stockade had been completed around its 26.5 acres, but no barracks or cooking facilities had been constructed. Nor did the prison staff have access to sufficient supplies to feed the number of prisoners who soon began arriving at the rate of 400 per day. By August 1864, the

23. Documented in Don Pettijohn, "African Americans at Andersonville" (unpublished paper, National Park Service, Andersonville National Historic Site, February 2006, http://home.nps.gov/ande/historyculture/people. htm).

prisoner population had grown to more than 32,000. Inevitably, this impossible situation turned into a humanitarian disaster. During fourteen months of operation, Confederate officials tallied 49,485 men incarcerated, of whom 12,912 (26 percent) died, most from disease, exposure, and malnutrition. Prison records also documented 329 successful escapes, while many more prisoners reportedly attempted escape, but were apprehended and returned.[24]

Compared with prisoner life aboard the Revolutionary War prison ship *Jersey*, incarceration in the Andersonville prison camp was probably as miserable but statistically less lethal. Estimates suggest that the *Jersey* may have contained 1,000 or more prisoners at a time in 1782, all crowded into the close quarters below the ship's deck. While reliable figures are lacking for overall mortality rates among *Jersey* prisoners, Dring's own crew from the *Chance* experienced over a 40 percent mortality rate, mostly from disease (see note 68 to Dring's narrative). In *Forgotten Patriots*, Edwin Burrows cites estimates made in the 1780s of between 4,000 and (precisely) 11,644 deaths on the *Jersey* during its "service" as a prison ship. Calculations based on British estimates of the cumulative number of prisoners on the *Jersey* and on a presumed mortality rate of 50 per-

24. See Raymond F. Baker, *Andersonville: The Story of a Civil War Prison Camp* (Washington, DC: National Park Service, 1972) (updated 2007). As in the Revolutionary War, a number of former Union prisoners subsequently told their Andersonville stories in print. Examples include Norton P. Chipman, *The Horrors of Andersonville Rebel Prison* (San Francisco, 1891); John L. Ransom, *Andersonville Diary*, initially published in 1881 (republished several times with the subtitle *Life Inside the Civil War's Most Infamous Prison* in 1963, 1986–with an introduction by Bruce Catton–and 1994-95); Ambrose Spencer, *A Narrative of Andersonville* (New York: Harper, 1866); R. Randolph Stevenson, *The Southern Side, or Andersonville Prison* (Baltimore, 1876). See also Ted Genoways and Hugh H. Genoways, eds., *A Perfect Picture of Hell: Eyewitness Accounts by Civil War Prisoners from the 12th Iowa* (Iowa City: University of Iowa Press, 2001).

cent, a figure thought possible or even low at the time, would yield a larger number of deaths, perhaps closer to 16,000.[25]

Confederate prisoners of war in Union prisons apparently experienced at least slightly better conditions than those endured by Union prisoners, although almost 26,000 Confederate prisoners died (compared to just over 30,000 Union soldiers in all Confederate prisons). One reason that better conditions existed in Union Civil War prisons was their greater ability to obtain food supplies from their respective hinterlands. By 1864, Georgia, like much of the South, was experiencing economic disaster, and shortages of food had become common, especially since most available food supplies were being sent north to feed hungry Confederate soldiers. Food for the huge numbers of Union prisoners in Confederate prisons was impossible to obtain, a situation parallel to that of the Americans incarcerated in British prison ships during the Revolutionary War.[26]

A fourth issue concerns the exchanging of privateer prisoners. In this matter again, the central government might have played a key role but failed to assume it. Congressional policy, established in 1776, was to exchange like for like, that is, soldier for soldier, sailor for sailor, rank for rank. This sounded equitable on paper and corresponded to British policy, but the Americans captured very few British seamen who might have been exchanged for the thousands of captured Americans, and they retained few of those they did capture. When, early in 1782, the British suggested an exchange of American privateersmen for British soldiers (whom they badly needed on the battlefield), General Washington flatly refused, unwilling to allow the British such a clear military advantage. This action must have looked very much like neglect to the prisoners

25. Burrows, *Forgotten Patriots*, 197–201.

26. See Baker, *Andersonville*, 16.

aboard the *Jersey*.[27] The matter never was settled on the central government level, so privateer prisoners had nowhere to look but to private sources of help, who in fact carried out a surprising number of exchanges directly with the British authorities.[28] Dring was the beneficiary of one such private exchange.

Examining the Civil War again, one reason that prison camps on both sides of the war were so crowded by 1864 was that neither General Grant nor General Lee could agree on a policy for mutual prisoner exchanges, but for entirely different reasons. Grant calculated strategically that one-for-one exchanges would be a bad deal, because emaciated Union exchangees would be incapable of returning to the front lines, while better fed Confederate exchangees would be prepared to return to active duty. Lee objected on principle, after the Emancipation Proclamation, to any one-on-one exchange that

27. Congressional policy on exchange was established on June 22, 1776 (quoted in Ford's notes, *Samuel Blackley Webb*, 2:25). Following this, the unsuccessful wrangling began for an agreement between American and British military officials. It was especially intense during 1782. See the following for letters by General Washington, David Sproat, Abraham Skinner, Admiral Digby, and others in Onderdonk, *Revolutionary Incidents*, 240–44; Banks, *David Sproat*, 59–80, 86–100; Dawson's appendix, Dring-Greene, *Recollections*, 131–41, 146–53; Dandridge, *American Prisoners*, 406–14, 424–31; Allen, *Naval History*, 637–38. See also George T. Curtis's "Report on Exchange of Prisoners." The English policy was more pragmatic. Although no national cartel could be arranged, since that would imply recognition of the United States, any "unofficial" exchanges were to be encouraged to return to the British forces the men they needed (see instructions to General Howe from Lord George Germain, February 1, 1776, quoted in Allen, *Naval History*, 621).

28. Newspapers of the time frequently noted the arrival of homeward-bound cartels. New London seems to have been most actively involved in private exchanges. See newspaper quotes in Onderdonk, *Revolutionary Incidents*, 229–31, 238–39; and in Bushnell's notes in *Adventures of Christopher Hawkins*, 259–62.

would free African American Union prisoners, thus recognizing them as free persons rather than runaway slaves. Unlike the
situation during the Revolutionary War, few if any informal,
private exchanges could be or were arranged.[29]

A fifth issue, the question of blame, must be considered.
Dring was a prisoner, so he blames mostly those who directly
caused his suffering, especially the guards. On a higher level, he
specifically blames David Sproat, commissary of prisoners, for
the fourth of July atrocities (see page 75), but declined to impli-
cate the top military commanders. Others not so personally
involved with the prison ships have agreed, supporting the
British high command's persistent contention that their policies were humane, but allowing (as the British officially did
not) that some of the underlings might have been more cor-
rupt (provision suppliers) or more cruel (guards) in practice
than policy dictated.[30] Other prisoners who wrote narratives
have felt, however, that the British followed a calculated policy of starvation and physical and mental abuse so that the prisoners would in desperation join the British service to obtain

29. See Pettijohn, "African Americans at Andersonville."

30. Representative views of this nature are expressed by Silas Talbot, and
especially by his editor, in *Silas Talbot*, 107–8; by Banks, *David Sproat*, who
attempts to resurrect David Sproat's ruined reputation (2); and by Dawson
in his introduction to Dring-Greene, *Recollections*, xviii. An interesting non-
naval incident supports this interpretation while also shedding light on
British-loyalist relations, and on questions of quasi-military legal status. One
Joshua Huddy, a captain in the Continental army, was captured in April 1782
by a band of quasi-military loyalist raiders called Associators, led by a Captain
Richard Lippincot, and sanctioned and nominally commanded by General
Henry Clinton. Instead of exchanging him, Lippincot had Huddy hanged in
retaliation for the recent killing by Americans of a loyalist named Philip
White. Even before General Washington's letter of protest and threatened
retaliation reached him, Clinton had moved to have Lippincot arrested for
court-martial on a charge of murder. Although Lippincot complained that
his court-martial was illegal, since he was not enrolled in the British army,

relief, or would be too weak to revolt or attempt escape, or would die, allowing space for more prisoners.[31]

Dring certainly leaned emotionally toward this view also, although he never expressed it as specifically as others. There is no evidence that this actually was a conscious British policy. What is clear is that whatever the British policy was, and however humane it sounded, the brutal reality of it made it appear, to Dring and others who shared his experience, to be a policy of calculated cruelty or even genocide. Of course, in the larger picture of the entire Revolutionary War, the British had no monopoly on policies and/or practices leading to misery and death. In this broader sense, blame must be shared by all participants on both sides, including many of those who became prisoners.

Edwin Burrows argues that, by the time some former *Jersey* prisoners wrote latter-day narratives about their experiences, their lives and values had been influenced by the burgeoning of early nineteenth-century evangelical Christianity. According to Burrows's interpretation, this led them, in essence, to blame their own human failings, rather than British cruelty, for the misery of their prisoner experiences. Burrows recognizes that Dring's narrative, written during the same time period (which he references in only the Dring–Greene published form),

the trial took place, and he was acquitted. See Sir Henry Clinton, *The American Rebellion.* . . . ed. William B. Willcox (New Haven: Yale University Press, 1954), 359–61; Larry G. Bowman, "The Court-Martial of Captain Richard Lippincot," *New Jersey History* 84 (1971): 23–36.

31. Alexander Coffin Jr., for example, was convinced "that there was a premeditated design to destroy as many Americans as they could on board of their Prison-ships." (See his letter to Dr. Samuel L. Mitchell printed in Dawson's appendix, Dring-Greene, *Recollections,* 186). See also the declaration of George Batterman made December 19, 1780, quoted in the *New-York Gazette and Weekly Mercury,* February 12, 1781, printed in Dandridge, *American Prisoners,* 443–44.

reflects a strong Christian belief but clearly places blame for his misery on British cruelty.[32]

Burrows also cites historical scholarship of the late 1970s that tends toward exonerating the British from engaging in premeditated, vindictively cruel and vicious practices on the prison ships. For instance, Larry G. Bowman maintains, in *Captive Americans*, that a study of British policy (as opposed to practice) reveals that it "could not be typified as cruel." Yet, he does concede that the practice of British policy "was not always handled well, and in many instances it lacked direction and effective control." More specifically, he recognizes that the overall actual conditions among American prisoners of the British were undeniably miserable, that "the prison ships were the most notorious aspect of the Revolution in regard to prisoners of war," and that "by far and away, the most infamous of the prison ships was the *Jersey*."[33]

Bowman further asserts that our inherited historical memory about American prisoners of the British has been biased because of an over-reliance on, and uncritical acceptance of, the published narratives of former prison ship prisoners, including that by Thomas Dring. As he sees it, "veterans of the British prisons were inclined to make extravagant and inaccurate statements which their editors frequently accepted at face value," that "Nearly all the literature . . . by veterans . . . reflects

32. See Burrows, *Forgotten Patriots*, 221–26. Burrows's larger, important point is that the memories of eyewitnesses who write narratives decades later about their experiences tend to evolve over the years, based on their later lives and experiences. Dring's emphasis in his narrative on events contemporary to his writing in 1824 (holding ceremonies to remember, erecting a monument, reinterring the bones) reveals his own preoccupation with the aftermath at least as much as the actuality of his prison experience years before.

33. Larry G. Bowman, *Captive Americans: Prisoners During the American Revolution* (Athens: Ohio University Press, 1976); see especially pp. 40–42 and 123–33.

a strong bias against Great Britain," and that "the men who wrote of their time in prison were not too well qualified to pinpoint the reasons and rationale behind Great Britain's policies concerning prisoners."[34]

Burrows refutes this scholarship as unhistorical revisionism precisely because it tends to discount the veracity of the narratives of eyewitnesses. Having argued elsewhere in his book that the early nineteenth-century prison ship narratives reflect values of evangelical Christianity, he supports the well-documented case that the narrative descriptions (including Dring's) of actual conditions and treatment by the British on the prison ships are mutually quite consistent and an accurate reflection of reality. Regardless of the debate over sources, Burrows and Bowman, along with most other historians and the narrative writers, agree that the actual conditions among prisoners on the *Jersey* were beyond miserable–they were deadly.[35]

In relation to the accuracy of Dring's memory, the duration of his imprisonment in his account deserves brief mention. He recollects his captivity to have lasted nearly five months. He leaves the impression that he and his fellows suffered for several agonizing months before they petitioned General Washington for exchange, sometime after the July 4 incidents. Actually the petition was delivered in early June, within two weeks after Dring's arrival on the *Jersey*. Furthermore, he was back in Providence by July 22, just over two months from the date of his incarceration on May 19. Clearly Dring's memory, filled with the horrors of the *Jersey*, stretched out the duration

<hr/>

34. Bowman, *Captive Americans*, vi, 123–24

35. See Bowman, *Captive Americans*; Beverly V. Baxter, "The American Revolutionary Experience: A Critical Study of the Diaries and Journals of American Prisoners During the Revolutionary Period" (PhD diss., University of Delaware, 1976); Robert J. Denn, "Prison Narratives of the American Revolution" (PhD diss., Michigan State University, 1980); Burrows, *Forgotten Patriots*, 248.

of his imprisonment to fit his concept of the magnitude of those horrors (for details see note 71 to Dring's narrative).

Finally, we must consider the role and importance, for Thomas Dring and for many others, of remembering and honoring those who had suffered and died as prisoners of war on the *Jersey*, on other prison ships, and, by extension, in other British prisons during the Revolutionary War. Dring's narrative proper ends with his return to Providence, Rhode Island. However, the manuscript contains a lengthy, fourteen-page appendix. After covering several topics briefly, he launches into a long and detailed description of the Tammany Society's efforts to collect and inter with honors the bones of the prisoners who had died on the prison ships and had been buried along the nearby Long Island shore. This entire account, which takes up eleven manuscript pages, was copied by Dring almost verbatim from a volume written for the Tammany Society in 1808. Because Dring did not write it, the description has been omitted from this printing. In other sections of the narrative, Dring incorporated additional segments from the same Tammany Society account, especially quotations from two orations, only one of which is identified by him. All these segments have been printed.[36]

The fact that Dring did not compose these paragraphs in the appendix himself does not detract from the importance they held for him. Evidently, a major purpose he cherished was to set down on paper an account of his personal experiences–and of later efforts to recognize the heroism of his and others' sacrifices–precisely so that their memories would not be forgotten and would be honored long into the future. These efforts continued for decades after his death in 1825, a year after he wrote his manuscript.

In 1791, a man named John Jackson acquired mill property on the edge of the mud flats, in which *Jersey's* (and other prison

36. See note 4 to Dring's narrative and page 121.

ship's) fatalities had been buried. He soon began discovering exposed human bones washed up around his property. After 1801, navy yard construction also began exposing bones. Jackson collected these bones. An active member of the Tammany Society of New York, he sought for political reasons to interest the organization in the bones. In 1808, the Tammany Society organized a large symbolic funeral procession with speeches, during which the bones Jackson had collected were deposited into a "vault" on his property. This event was part of an unsuccessful effort by the Tammany Society to convince Congress to finance a fitting monument. Dring's manuscript contains passages copied from the recorded speeches of this day. About thirty years later, another Tammany Society leader purchased the land and built a "chamber" over the vault. Meanwhile, efforts continued to finance a monument.[37]

Finally, in 1873, the accumulated bones of dead *Jersey* prisoners were ceremoniously reinterred in a crypt intended to reside under a monument. This monument was to be located within the new Washington Park, designed in 1867 by Frederick Law Olmstead (who had already designed Central Park on Manhattan and was then beginning to design Prospect Park in Brooklyn) and his colleague Calvert Vaux. The park is located above Wallabout Bay at the site of the American Revolutionary War Fort Putnam, constructed in 1776 under the command of Major General Nathanael Greene (for whom the park was renamed in 1897). After reinforcement during the War of 1812, the fort was subsequently abandoned.[38]

---

37. See Armbruster, *Wallabout Prison Ships*, 22; and Burrows, *Forgotten Patriots*, 205–40. See page 124 and note 4 to Dring's narrative for Dring's copied excerpts from the speeches at the 1808 event.

38. The most useful summary sources on the history and timeline of the interment and monument are found at http://www.flickr.com/photos/wal-lyg/2433153635/and at http://homepages.rootsweb.ancestry.com/~pro-maine/martyrs/Monument-timeline.html. See also Burrows, *Forgotten Patriots*, 205–40.

Not until 1908 was the Martyr's Monument finally erected in the center of the park. The monument consists of a wide, monumental staircase leading up to a single, central Doric column rising 148 feet above the park with a large bronze urn on top. The four corners of the monument area were decorated with large bronze eagles. After many years of neglect, the entire monument was renovated in 2008, and a solar light was installed in the urn to provide a "perpetual flame" over the monument.[39]

This book presents for the first time Thomas Dring's story in his own words as he wrote it. A portion of the Appendix that he copied from other sources and which does not materially contribute to the narrative has been ommited as mentioned above; the identity of this material is indicated in the notes. In addition, the editor has made other decisions about how to present the manuscript in print. The poetry included in the manuscript, all of which is printed here, was also largely borrowed, as Dring acknowledges (see note 9 to Dring's narrative and page 121). The poet is Philip Freneau, who was himself a prison ship captive in 1780. Poetry not identified to be by Freneau (except for a verse on page 119) is apparently original verse by Dring himself.

Dring's manuscript has been reproduced here essentially as he wrote it, with the exceptions noted above. The following rules have been observed in the editing process. All spelling, capitalization, and punctuation have been modernized. Sentence structure has been supplied where needed. Grammar

39. See New York City Department of Parks and Recreation, Fort Greene Park, http://www.nycgovparks.org/parks/FortGreenePark/pressrelease/20782.

has been corrected only where corrections were slight or were necessary to clarify the meaning. Bracketed words have been entered to clarify meaning.

Dring's descriptive headings, such as "The Approach and Entry on Board the *Jersey*," which in the manuscript appear at the top of the manuscript's pages, are each recorded once at the head of their corresponding sections. In places where the heading is divided across a page, the division is indicated by brackets.

The editor's notes are meant to provide explanation, historical perspective, and details of points made in the editor's introduction. No attempt has been made to analyze in detail the differences between the original Dring text and the previously published Dring–Greene text. Biographical information has been supplied where such information could be found. Most of Dring's fellow prisoners, even some he recalls as being prominent citizens, have long since been forgotten in the pages of recorded history.

In considerable measure, Thomas Dring has accomplished his purpose of preserving the memory of British prison ship life–and death–during the Revolutionary War. Nearly two centuries after Dring penned his narrative, this book continues to further his cause. Combined with the recent renovation of the Monument to the Martyrs in Fort Greene Park, Brooklyn, this book helps remind us of both the inhuman horrors and the heroic sacrifices spawned by war.

RECOLLECTIONS OF LIFE ON THE PRISON SHIP *Jersey* in 1782

THOMAS DRING

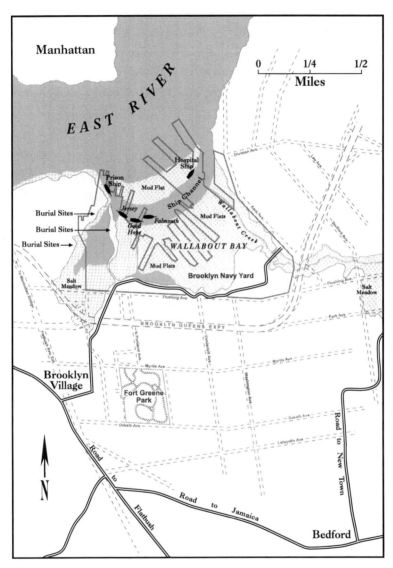

The site of British prison ships at Wallabout Bay, New York, in 1782 with a modern overlay, including the Brooklyn Navy Yard and Fort Greene Park, site of the Martyr's Monument.

INTRODUCTION

Among the many events which took place during the Revolutionary War from its commencement to its termination [are] the cruelties inflicted upon that unfortunate class of men who had the misfortune to be numbered among the prisoners [of the British] and more particularly those whom the dreadful chance of war had placed on board their prison ships at New York.[1] The theme has been occasionally introduced upon the anniversary of our independence, among other events of our revolutionary contest, on the 4th of July, when an oration has been acclaimed and, suited to the occasion, the suffering and cruelties afflicted upon the American prisoners have been feebly dwelt upon. A narration of those events has given umbrage to some cold hearted wretches who have even said that the tale was not founded in truth or [was] exaggerated, and [that] the motive in even mentioning the circumstance was purely to irritate their friends, the English. That such wretches are still among us and do encumber the American

1. New York was a center of British activity throughout most of the war. It also became the most important British prison location in North America, though prisons were also maintained at Charleston, South Carolina, Newport, Rhode Island, Halifax, Bermuda, and the West Indies. At various times more than a dozen different ships were used as prisons by the British at New York. None enjoyed a positive reputation, but the *Jersey* earned the most infamous rating among Americans. See note 5.

soil is to be lamented, but contention with this class of people is not my present object. Those remarks, however, have induced me to give a feeble description of the treatment of the prisoners who were on board the prison ships, a narrative which is founded in facts.

The writer was twice a prisoner during the war and more than four months at each time, first on board the *Good Hope* prison ship in the year 1779 then lying in the North [Hudson] River opposite New York, from which he made his escape to the Jersey shore. But [he] shall pass over those events and confine himself more particularly to the treatment and occurrences on board that sink of all human misery called the old *Jersey*. I was nearly five months on board of this dismal hulk in the year 1782 and was an eye witness to the unspeakable sufferings of this wretched class of American prisoners,[2] a description of which will hereafter be feebly described, but [will] fall far short of the reality. It is but justice that our sufferings should be handed down to posterity. It will show to future generations what their ancestors endured during this contest.

The writer is now far advanced in years and the only survivor (with the exception of two) [of those] who were taken with him at the time he here alludes to, out of sixty-five. I often pass the descendants of my old companions in captivity. It always brings to my mind that "your father was once my companion and fellow sufferer in prison" and perhaps that "I saw him breathe his last and assisted at his interment at the Wallabout," a circumstance probably wholly unknown to them at this time.

My principal motive in committing our sufferings on board the old *Jersey* prison ship at New York to writing was to strengthen my memory and recollection of the scene and the time, and although more than forty years have elapsed since

2. He was actually on the *Jersey* for only about two months. See note 71.

that event,[3] it seems but as yesterday to me, and such is the impression it has upon my mind that it can never be obliterated while I have the sense of memory. In a short time there will be no one upon the face of the earth to relate the tale. There are still many living among us who, although they were not among the sufferers themselves, are still well knowing to the circumstances which I am about to relate and have been personally acquainted with the fallen victims.

There are thousands who died there, "and their names are not known . . . . They suffered, when no eye could admire, and no voice praise" [Fay, 59].[4] Shall not their names and their virtues be told to posterity? And it is only from the few that still survive that posterity can be made acquainted with their deplorable condition. The very name of the old *Jersey* seemed

---

3. Dring is writing early in 1824 at the age of sixty-five. He was twenty-three years old when captured and imprisoned on the *Jersey*.

4. This is the first of several passages Dring incorporated (without identification except for the one on pages 8–9, "oration") into his text from *An Account of the Interment of the Remains of 11,500 American Seamen. . . .* by [Jacob Vandervoort] for the Tammany Society (New York: Frank, White, 1808). The passages come from three sources within the book, and each one is identified in Dring's text as explained below, along with the page number on which the passage occurs in the *Account*:

Descriptions by Vandervoort are labeled [Vandervoort].

Quotations from the oration by Joseph D. Fay on April 13, 1808, at the ceremony for the laying of the cornerstone of a tomb for the remains of those who died on the prison ships, are labeled [Fay].

Quotations from the oration by Dr. Benjamin De Witt on May 26, 1808, at the interment of the remains, are labeled [De Witt].

Bracketed words in these passages show significant changes of wording Dring made as he copied from Vandervoort's *Account*. Otherwise, these passages have been printed here unedited, as they were originally published in the *Account*, including a few places where Dring clearly miscopied. In other passages scattered throughout the text, Dring lifted words and phrases, or more freely paraphrased from the *Account*.

to strike a terror to all those whose necessities induced them
to venture upon the ocean. The mortality that prevailed on
board this hulk was well known throughout our then bleeding
country.5 To be an inmate in this infernal place of confinement
was considered by all who had the misfortune to be placed on
board of her as a certain death from which they could not
expect to escape. With those impressions upon our minds, the
crew with whom I was captured, composed of about sixty-five
men and boys, in the short space of four or five months lost
many of our men, as will hereafter be related, from pestilence
and cruel treatment on board those "floating dungeons, the
hearts of whose keepers must indeed have delighted in the
'luxury of woes'; the bodies of our countrymen, having gone
through the preparatory stages of suffering and death, were
taken ashore at the Wallabout" [Vandervoort, 4],* the place of
interment.

How many perished on board those prison ships and how
many were thus carried to this modern Golgotha cannot be
accurately stated. It is ascertained, however, and that with as
much precision as the nature of the case will admit of, that
upwards of ten thousand died on board those hulks at New
York.6 They had at the same time three hospital ships near the

*The Wallabout is on Long Island shore near the Navy Yard. [Footnote
by Dring. See note 8.]

5. The degree of the *Jersey's* bad reputation stems largely, of course, from its
awful conditions and high mortality rate. However, the fact that for more
than three years (1780–83), this particular vessel received almost all of the
incoming privateer and naval prisoners, after which some were transferred to
other prison or hospital ships, created among thousands of prisoners a dis-
tinct and lasting first impression of the *Jersey* over the other prison ships.

6. On May 18, 1783, an unidentified "AMERICAN" wrote a letter to the
nation's newspaper editors stating that "11,644 American prisoners have suf-

old *Jersey* for our reception, all equally pestilential, namely that of the *Scorpion*, the *Strombolo*, and the *Hunter*, hospital ships which were also graves to nearly all who entered their mansions. A more minute description I shall endeavor to give in my present narrative. Previous to relating our sufferings on board the old *Jersey* prison ship, it may be necessary to give a description of her.[7] She had been a British ship of the line rated in the register as a sixty-four gun ship but generally carried seventy-four guns. Being old, she was, it seems, in the early part of the war entirely dismantled and converted into a store ship and lay in the East River at New York, and in the year 1780 she was made use of as a prison ship and remained as such during the whole period of the Revolution. Fearful from the infection arising from this nauseous hulk, they caused her to be removed to the Wallabout upon the Long Island shore, a solitary and

fered death . . . on board the filthy and malignant British prison-ship, called the Jersey" (quoted in Onderdonk, *Revolutionary Incidents,* 245). Most writers on the subject, including Dring, have felt that this figure is too high for the *Jersey* alone, but that it may be approximately accurate for all the deaths on all the prison ships at New York. Still, the *Jersey* contributed at least its share. If one uses Dring's estimated average of five deaths per day, which is approximately corroborated by other narratives, and calculates that rate for three years, the total is nearly fifty-five hundred deaths. See also page 81 and note 53.

7. The 1,000-ton warship *Jersey* (of 60 guns according to British records) was built in 1736. After duty in the Mediterranean, West Indies, and Newfoundland, she was laid up in 1747 as unfit for active service. Refitted again when French hostilities broke out, she served in the Mediterranean from 1756 to 1763, and again from 1766 to 1769, when she was once more laid up. But she was resurrected again in 1776, and sent to New York to serve as a hospital and then, after 1779, as a prison ship. Her masts were removed there, and in 1783 the British abandoned her to rot. See descriptions in Dawson's editorial appendix, Dring-Greene, *Recollections,* 196–98; and in Bushnell's editorial notes in *Adventures of Christopher Hawkins,* 206–14.

unfrequented place.[8] Here no one passed her, and no pitying eye could dwell for a moment upon this heinous hulk whose bowels contained some of the best blood of our country. Here was moored with chain cables, without mast or rudder, the old *Jersey*. Her former ports had been all strongly fastened in. Through her sides at about ten feet apart were square holes cut about twenty inches square across which thick bars of iron were placed at right angles, leaving four small spaces which admitted light by day and [were a] breathing space at night. The filth which had been from time to time collected upon her sides from the bends upward had been permitted to remain there for years, nor could all the waters from heaven remove it. As the prisoners occupied two decks, there were of course two tiers of those barred breathing holes fore and aft. The ship had nothing standing but the bowsprit and the derrick for taking in the water. [There was] no one solitary sound but that of the ship's bell and the groans of the dying victims.

Here lay "the black hulk of the *Jersey* Prison-ship" and the equally heart appalling view of the hospital ships "surrounded with 'a close incumbent cloud' of pestilence–filled with foul and suffocating vapors–and echoing with the cries, and the groans, and the supplications of distress. Like a huge monster of the deep, she devoured her thousands at a meal, and rapidly disgorged the half-consumed and mangled carcasses. There in her putrefactive bowels wallowed in filth a crowd of living men, amongst the dying and the dead–There the sun-beam never entered, and the zephyr never blew– . . . . The grief-worn prisoner lay without a bed . . ., without a pillow to support his

8. The Wallabout was at that time a bay and tidal flat on the Long Island shore, northeast of the town of Brooklyn, across from New York. Subsequently part of the area became the site of the Brooklyn Navy Yard. Dawson spells the name Wale Bogt, and suggests that it is a Dutch name meaning "the bend of the inner harbor" (Dawson's note in Dring-Greene, *Recollections*, 27).

aching head—the tattered garment torn from his meager frame, and vermin preying on his flesh." (oration) [De Witt, 86]

> *No masts or sails [this] crowded ship adorn,*
> *Dismal to view, neglected and forlorn!*
> *//*
> *Hail, dark abode! what can with thee compare—*
> *Heat, sickness, famine, death, and stagnant air—*
> [Freneau][9]

9. This is the first of many segments of poetry that Dring incorporated into his text. As he explains in his appendix (page 121), most of them were written by Philip Freneau, who turned real-life stories of prison ship life (including briefly, his own) into a lengthy, emotionally compelling poem titled "The British Prison Ship." The poem was published in 1781 and was extremely popular among American patriots. Dring states that he has occasionally changed Freneau's wording where necessary to fit the meaning of his text. Dring's words in these cases are indicated with brackets. The editor has also corrected Freneau's poetry from Dring's slightly inaccurate recollection to conform to the original as printed in *Poems of Philip Freneau,* 2:18–39. In the text, Freneau's poetry is identified by the editor with [Freneau] after each passage. Couplets found together in the Dring text but unconnected in the original are separated by the editor with the sign //. Unidentified poetry was apparently written by Dring himself, except for one passage on page 119.

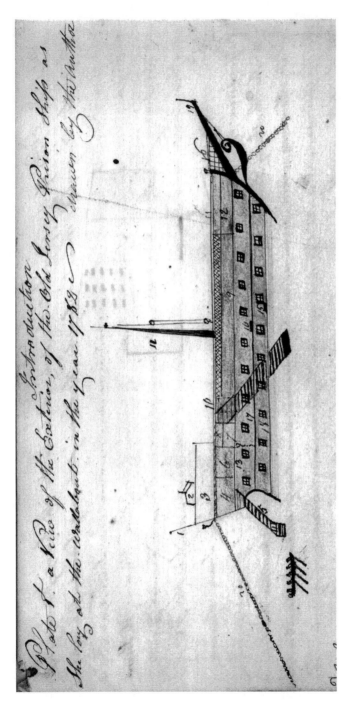

"Plate 1. A view of the exterior of the old *Jersey* prison ship as she lay at the Wallabout in the year 1782, drawn by the author."
(Rhode Island Historical Society)

Plate 1. A view of the exterior of the old *Jersey* prison ship as she lay at the Wallabout in the year 1782, drawn by the author.

References:

1. The flag staff. N.B., it was seldom colors were set, only for signals etc.
2. An awning or tent of canvas used in warm weather by the guards.
3. Quarterdeck and a barricade about 10 feet high, a door on each side, and loopholes.
4. The ship's officers' cabin, under the quarterdeck.
5. The accommodation ladder, on the starboard side, for ship's use (officers).
6. The steerage, or room for the sailors belonging to the ship *Jersey*.
7. The cook room for the ship's crew, guards, etc.
8. The sutler's room, where things were sold to the prisoners through a hole in the bulkhead.
9. The upper deck and spar deck, where the prisoners walked.
10. The gangway ladder, on the larboard side, for prisoners occasionally.
11. The derrick, on the starboard side, to take in water etc.
12. The galley or great copper, for the prisoners' cooking, under the forecastle.
13. The gun room, where the prisoners lived (that is, the officers).
14. and 15. The hatchways on each deck leading below, where the prisoners lived.
16. Necessary, in the head rails.
17. and 18. Between decks, where the prisoners were confined at night.
19. The bowsprit.
20. Chain cables, by which the ship was moored.

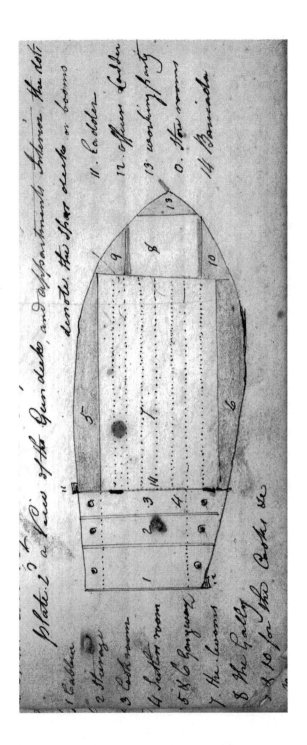

"Plate 2. A view of the gun [or upper] deck and apartments' interior. The dots denote the spar deck or booms."
(*Rhode Island Historical Society*)

Plate 2. A view of the gun [or upper] deck and apartments' interior. The dots denote the spar deck or booms.

[References:]
  1. Cabin
  2. Steerage
  3. Cook room
  4. Sutler's room
  5. and 6. Gangway
  7. The booms
  8. The galley
  9. and 10. For the cooks etc.
11. Ladder
12. Officers' ladder
13. Working party
o Store rooms
14. Barricade

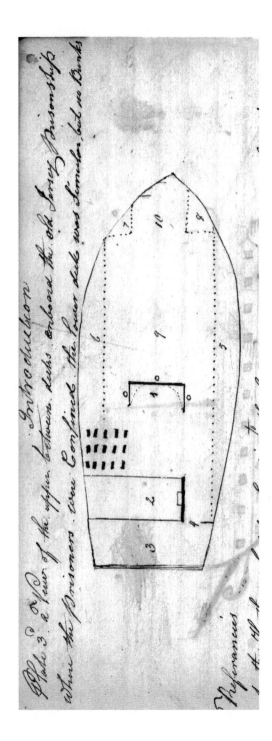

"Plate 3. A view of the upper between decks on board the old *Jersey* prison ship, where the prisoners were confined. The lower deck was similar, but [had] no bunks." (*Rhode Island Historical Society*)

Plate 3. A view of the upper between decks on board the old *Jersey* prison ship, where the prisoners were confined. The lower deck was similar, but [had] no bunks.

References:

1. The hatchway ladder leading to the lower deck, railed around on three sides.

2. The steward's room, from which we received our daily allowance through a hole (▭)

3. The gun room, where the officers among the prisoners resided.

4. The doorway, the gun room being the extreme after part of the ship.

5., 6., 7., 8. The arrangement for the prisoners, chests and boxes upon a line about ten feet from the side of the ship behind which messes assembled.

9. and 10. Where many hammocks were hung by night, but always down by day to afford room to walk etc. between decks.

o o o Several tubs for the occasional *use* of the prisoners by night.

▬ ▬ ▬ Bunks on the larboard side for the sick until removed to the hospital ships.

The prisoners were removed to the hospital ships provided they were able to crawl up to the head of the accommodation ladder, where to be examined by a doctor's mate. If he was judged to be a candidate for the hospital ship, he was immediately assisted into the boat in waiting, assisted by the nurses, not, however, without the loss of all his effects. If he was not able to ascend for examination, his case was considered as too far gone, and he was left to expire where he was. The doctor's mate generally came on board in the forenoon from one of the hospital ships (I think it was the *Hunter*). This ship appeared to be a kind of depot for everything appertaining to the sick and the dead. From her came a boat upon signal given from the ferry or the other ships. This boat, rowed by four men and a steerer, was ever on duty from ship to ship as occasion might require. She took the dead on shore for interment, and the steersman had among us (the prisoners) the name of "the Sexton." There was a small hut near the landing place. This contained the handbarrows [and] shovels, and the Sexton (so called) kept the key. That apparatus was in use every day.

Having given the reader some idea of the hulks and their appendages, I shall proceed to give a feeble description of our treatment in the following narrative, to the best of my quotation.

[NARRATIVE]

Sir:

In compliance with your request wishing me to give a statement of such facts as I might be acquainted with respecting the treatment and the situation of the American prisoners during the Revolutionary War,[10] so far as I was an eye witness during my own confinement on board their prison ships at New York and particularly that of the old *Jersey*, in order that you might have a better conception of our situation and place of confinement, I have by way of introduction annexed a drawing of this odious hulk, an exterior and interior view, together with some observations upon the subject, which I thought might be necessary. I have only to add [my] being personally acquainted with the whole treatment from sorrowful experience in two cases of captivity and confinement on board those sinks of human misery, that is, once on board the *Good Hope* in 1779[11] and again on board the old *Jersey* in the year 1782, and [I was] nearly five months on board of each of them, which was time sufficient to make every observation you require, and in order to be more particular in this narrative, it may be necessary to state that I was captured [the second time] in a privateer called

10. There is no further evidence that the narrative is a letter written to answer one person's request. Dring's reason for artificially choosing this format is unclear, but does not seem of great significance.

11. The *Good Hope* was used as a prison ship from early 1779 until March 5, 1780, on which date it burned, apparently at the hands of its prisoners, who successfully saved themselves. See *An Appeal to the Congress of the United States from the Society of Old Brooklynites, for the Erection of a Monument. . . .* (Brooklyn, NY: 1890), 13; an article in the *New York Royal Gazette*, March 8, 1780, printed in Onderdonk, *Revolutionary Incidents*, 231; David Sproat to Abraham Skinner, January 29, 1781, printed in Banks, *David Sproat*, 43.

the *Chance* commanded by Daniel Aborn,[12] owned in Providence by Messrs. Clark and Nightingale.[13]

The [ship] was officered and manned principally from Providence and its vicinity. The *Chance* was a new vessel and on her first cruise. [She] mounted twelve six-pound cannon with a complement of about sixty-five men and sailed on a cruise sometime in May 1782 and was captured in a few days after our sailing by a British ship of war called the *Belisarius* commanded by Captain Graves mounting twenty-six guns.[14]

12. Daniel Aborn, a resident of Pawtuxet, was born at Newport into the prominent Rhode Island family of Captain Joseph Aborn on July 1, 1749. He married Mary Arnold of Cranston in 1769. A sea captain before the Revolution, he turned to privateering during the war. In 1780 he commanded the *Chance* on an apparently successful privateering voyage (see Edward Field, *State of Rhode Island and Providence Plantations*. . . . [Boston: Mason Publishing, 1902], 2:427). In 1782 he was not so lucky. After the war he returned to the merchant service. In December 1783 he sailed for the West Indies. His ship was never heard from again (see Dawson's appendix, Dring-Greene, *Recollections*, 158; *The History of Rhode Island and Providence Plantations: Biographical* (New York: American Historical Society, 1920), 1:204. Concerning Captain Aborn, see also pages 93, 99–103, and note 64.

13. The firm of Clark and Nightingale was one of the most prominent merchant companies in Providence at the time. During the Revolution the firm competed in privateering and cooperated in shipping needed supplies into Providence with John Brown's firm (see Field, State of Rhode Island, 424–30, 447; James B. Hedges, *The Browns of Providence: Colonial Years* (Cambridge, MA: Harvard University Press, 1952). The two owners, John Innes Clark (1745–1808) and Joseph Nightingale (1749–1797), were also prominent citizens in Providence public life (see William R. Staples, *Annals of the Town of Providence* (Providence, RI: Knowles and Vose, 1843).

14. The *Chance* sailed from Providence on about May 6, 1782. She was captured on May 11, and by May 19 the prisoners had been put on board the *Jersey* (see the *Providence Gazette*, July 27, 1782). The *Belisarius*, built as a frigate at Boston early in 1781, was captured by the British later in the same year while privateering. She was promptly commissioned into the British

It is not necessary to dwell upon the subject of our capture in this place. Suffice it to say, we were captured in the night, conveyed on board as prisoners, and the next morning put in irons. The next day they captured [both] another American privateer, a brig called the *Samson* of twelve guns belonging to New London (or Stonington) commanded by Captain _____ Brooks,[15] and a schooner from Warren, R. I., a merchant vessel commanded by Captain Charles Collins.[16] All of those captures were made on soundings south of Long Island shore, and [with] the prisoners, upwards of one hundred thirty, they then made their way for New York with their prizes. We were all put in irons except the principal officers, a measure of good precaution on their part for which no blame could be attached. We were kept down in the cable tier (so called), admitting, however, part of us to go upon deck by day at a time.

The *Belisarius* returns to New York

Having so many prisoners on board, as before mentioned, they made the best of their way for New York, where we arrived in a few days and came to anchor abreast of the city in the East River. Our situation for some time past had not, to be sure,

navy and was used rather successfully against other American privateers. Her captain, Richard Graves, was the son of a clergyman from Derby County, England. See Dawson's appendix, Dring-Greene, *Recollections*, 194–95; Bushnell's notes in *Adventures of Christopher Hawkins*, 196–89, 200–2.

15. Of the *Samson* and her captain we know nothing except that she did sail from New London, and that Captain Brooks did not survive his captivity (see page 48).

16. The vessel was the *Swordfish*. Charles Collins was paroled quickly, because, Dring suspects, his cargo was a valuable deckload of livestock. See page 98. He also signed the controversial statement concerning conditions on the *Jersey* on June 22, 1782. See note 64.

been a very desirable one, but as bad as it was, it was far preferable to what we expected hereafter and to our grief soon experienced.

A signal was made denoting that they had prisoners on
board. Soon after, two large gondolas (or boats) came alongside of the ship, on board of which was David Sproat, commissary of prisoners.[17] This miscreant was an American refugee
[loyalist] and universally detested. We now for the first time
saw his frightful face with abhorrence.

> *But, sir, you might have search'd creation round*
> *Ere such another [ruffian] could be found–*
> [Freneau]

We were now admitted on deck and loosened from our irons
and ordered into the boats, which being accomplished, we put
off under a guard of marines from the ship toward our much
dreaded place of confinement, which was not then in view.
Passing along under the Long Island shore [with] the tide
against us, we made little progress. Sproat ordered us to apply
ourselves to the oars, but having no inclination to expedite our
passage, we declined obeying him. He tauntingly replied, "I
will soon fix you, my lads." We soon, however, doubled a point,
which gave us a view of the Wallabout where lay the black

17. David Sproat was a Scotsman who had come to Philadelphia in 1760.
After the war broke out, he took the loyalist side and joined the British army
at New York in 1777. His first major responsibility was dealing with the army
prisoners of the Battle of Brandywine. Later he handled the Saratoga and
Yorktown prisoner exchanges. In October 1779 he also took charge of all
naval prisoners. He performed all these duties from headquarters at New
York. After the war, back in Scotland, he successfully petitioned Congress for
reimbursement of private expenses he claimed to have incurred caring for the
prisoners. He died in 1799 at the age of sixty-four. See Banks, *David Sproat*,
for a very sympathetic treatment of the man and his work during the
Revolution, 3–4, 26, 104–27, and Dawson's note in Dring-Greene,
Recollections, 26.

hulk of the old *Jersey* together with her satellites, the three hospital ships. The wretch of a commissary then exultingly said, "There, rebels, there is a cage for you." Oh, how I wished to have this inhuman scoundrel upon the turf and with my heel have crushed the serpent's head.

Every eye was instantly turned from the odious sight. We, however, had a glance at the hulk and observed a multitude of moving men upon her upper deck. Many had gotten upon the bowsprit by way (as I afterwards understood) of getting without the limits [of the guards?]. It was now nearly the setting sun, and before we got alongside, every man had disappeared except the sentinels upon the gangways. Some of the prisoners, previous to their being turned below, saw us coming toward them. They waved their hats and seemed to say "approach us not", at least we so construed it, and we afterwards found it verified.

> *Conveyed [on board], we found, at length, too late,*
> *That death was better than the prisoner's fate;*
> *There doom'd to famine, shackles and despair,*
> *Condemn'd to breathe a foul, infected air.*
> [Freneau]

The Approach and Entry on Board the *Jersey*

We had now reached the accommodation ladder, upon the larboard side of the Jersey, which we ascended to the gangway and [passed] through the barricade door upon the same side, where our bags (if we had any) were examined, and if no arms, weapons, or money was discovered, we were permitted to take them with us. Our names and capacity being enrolled, we passed through the other barricade door, upon the starboard side, down the ladder leading to the main hatchway. I was in no haste to enter upon this ceremony and deterred it as long as possible. It had now become nearly dark, and lanterns had become necessary for examination during this time.

My situation on board the boat came exactly in right con-
tact with one of the air ports, from which place came a current
of foul air. It was of a nature to which I had become accustomed on a former captivity on board the *Good Hope* and at
once brought to my recollection the disgusting smell, after a
lapse of three years or more, though with accumulated nau-
seousness which it's impossible for me to describe, and while
here in waiting, we had some conversation with the prisoners
through the gratings, whom we could not distinctly discern.
After some questions on their part as to our capture and where
we belonged etc., one observed to us that it was a lamentable
sight to them to see so many young men with health upon
their countenances about to enter their infernal place of abode.
He observed that death had no relish for their skeleton carcasses and that he would now have a feast upon fresh comers. This,
however, said he, may have a tendency to prolong our existence here, of which we already tired. This discourse was hard-
ly calculated to afford us any kind consolation, which we, alas,
to our grief soon found to be the case.

> *Better to sleep on ocean's deepest bed,*
> *At once destroy'd and number'd with the dead,*
> *Than thus to perish in the face of day*
> *Where twice ten thousand deaths one death delay.*
> [Freneau]

It now became necessary for me to ascend and pass through
the same ceremony, which I did with little detention and [got]
permission to take with me my bag of clothes, and, passing
through the other door, as before mentioned, down to the
hatchway, which was still open, through a guard of soldiers, [I]
joined the dismal throng.

> *[They] pointed to the stairs that led below*
> *To damps, disease, and varied shapes of woe–*

Down to the gloom I took my pensive way,
Along the decks the dying captives lay.
[Freneau]

The First Night's Scene

The gratings being now laid, I seated myself near the hatch-way, grasping my bag by way of security. I here reflected upon the horrors of the scene and the prospect before me. Separated from my companions by darkness, I had no one to speak to during this dreadful night, surrounded by I knew not whom, except that they were fellow sufferers with myself. Dismal sounds from every direction greeting my ear, a nauseous and deadly smell entering at every breath I drew, together with the suffocating heat, almost deprived me of life. I employed some time in disencumbering myself of some of my apparel which I had put on by way of security before I entered the ship, say three shirts, etc. This I found absolutely necessary and was willing to hazard the loss of my clothes for the benefit of a little respiration.

Throughout my frame I felt its deadly heat,
I felt my pulse with quicker motions beat.
[Freneau]

In this my wakeful condition, I observed the glimmering of light through the iron grating. I thought it would be a luxury indeed if I could obtain a situation near this desirable place to breathe the sweet air, and with my bag closely clinched, I made the advance toward this wished for place, not, however, without the curses of those whom in my progress I had disturbed by attempting to get over them. By perseverance I, however, got near my desired spot but now found it already occupied, and no persuasion could induce them to relinquish it for a moment. It was their enclosure by chest, as will be soon described, a circumstance to which I was then unacquainted.

The night was now far advanced, and I waited until the return of day with sorrowful forebodings. The light at length appeared but returned only to present new objects of disease and wretchedness, unknown visages now appearing with death and famine upon their pallid faces. My comrades or former shipmates were all lost among the multitude, and it was not until we were permitted to ascend the deck at 8 o'clock the next morning that I saw a face that I knew. Pale and meager, they crept along to view another sun and again to pass a day of wretchedness and woe.

> *But what to them is morn's delightful ray,*
> *Sad and distressful as the close of day,*
> *//*
> *O may I ne'er review these dire abodes,*
> *These piles for slaughter, floating on the floods–*
> [Freneau]

The First Day's Scene

After passing a restless night, the horrors of which cannot be described, the return of morning discovered new objects in our view, disgusting to our sight. A multitude of miserable wretches in tattered garments and pale visages presented themselves, crowding upon the deck to breathe a fresh air. I now and then saw a ruddy and healthy complexion, which I recognized to be one of my late fellow prisoners on board of the *Belisarius*–how different in appearance to those miserable objects who had survived or combated with death and disease. They, when they entered those dreadful abodes, were as healthy as we were at present.

Let me "tell you that he who had breathed the pure breezes of the ocean, and had danced lightly in the flower-scented air of the meadow and the hill, was on a sudden transferred to the pent-up air of a Prison-ship, pregnant with putrid fever, and deadly with nauseous contagion . . . . He lingered out the tedious, weary day, and anxious, dreadful night, hopeful that death would kindly come and release him from misery. He fainted in the sultry heat of summer, and shivered in the merciless blast of winter . . . . It is no fable. Alas! it is too faithful a picture" [Fay, 57–58] and the dismal prospect before us filled our hearts with dread.

I had been tormented through the night with what I apprehended was vermin, and as soon as I got upon deck, I found my black silk handkerchief that I then wore around my neck was well spotted with vermin. Having never before had or seen anything of this kind, the first sight of [them] made me shudder, particularly as I knew they were hereafter to be my constant companions and everlasting tormentors while I should remain on board the hulk, which I concluded, however, could not be of long duration, as death must unavoidably soon be my fate.

Another sad object soon presented itself to my view. It was a man with the small pox, and [I] very soon discovered that I was surrounded by many with the same disorder. It became absolutely necessary to be immediately inoculated (as I had never had it), and having no one to do it for me, it was my task to stand my own doctor, and [I] soon found a man full with it and applied to my fellow prisoner, though a stranger, for this favor of taking the matter from him, to which he complied and observed that he thought it a necessary precaution, as he had taken it the natural way himself, though he was then in a fair way of recovery, and further observed that very fortunately my present situation on board the *Jersey* was a most excellent place for diet, as it was extremely moderate.

Small Pox

I had no instrument but a pin to perform this operation with, and, having scratched my skin with it between the thumb and forefinger, I applied some of the matter and bound it up, and the next morning it had begun to fester, a sure presage of its having taken effect. Many others of the newcomers were using the same precaution. As to the small pox, I have only to observe that I here had it very favorably without the advice or assistance of any physician whatever and attended with no expense. I often since (after a lapse of more than forty years) look at the scar it has left upon my hand. It brings fresh to my recollection the dread upon my mind upon that occasion, but through the kind protection of divine Providence, I not only recovered from this loathsome disorder but also avoided every malady prevailing on board this dreadful hulk during the whole of my confinement there during the summer season "when the [heat] rages with relentless fury, when a pure air is especially essential to health, and even the bosom of indolent ease, pants to catch it from . . . the *hill*" [Fay, 54].

We were barred down by night. In vain did the fainting and exhausted prisoner seek for a breathing space through the scanty bars of his prison. Those places were already occupied for the same purpose. He was left to grope his way in utter darkness along the crowded deck, already quite encumbered by a mass of almost suffocated wretches in the same condition. "As yet health blooms on his cheek, and the vigour of a robust constitution gives grace to his manly form. With an eye of proud disdain he looks upon his tyrant keepers, and . . . believes that the oppressor's arm can never subdue him. Alas! the hour rapidly approaches when his manly form shall wither on the shore–and dogs and eagles shall devour it" [Fay, 57–58].

> *The various horrors of these hulks to tell,*
> *These Prison Ships where pain and horror dwell,*
> *//*
> *When [four] long months in [this] dark hulk [I] lay,*
> *Barr'd down by night, and fainting all the day.*
> [Freneau]

We had now fasted nearly twenty-four hours and knew not how to obtain a morsel of bread. For my own part, I had the precaution to put a few biscuits in my bag, which I took at the time of our capture and had not occasion to use while on board the Belisarius, so that I did not suffer much myself and gave some to my comrades. We could not be benefited by our allowance in time on the first day to have cooked it, not having been formed into regular messes and numbered agreeable to the regulation of the ship, which was made known to us and soon complied with by selecting our mess mates composed of six, and the next morning we drew our scanty pittance.

The Gun Room and Messing

There was no partiality whatever shown by our foes toward us poor prisoners. How or by whom taken made no difference with them. If taken in arms or from our firesides was all the same. Once we had the dreadful misfortune to be enclosed within those dreary abodes of this hulk, all was upon a footing as respected our fare, our treatment, our allowance, and the quality thereof was the same.

I have before stated that the very extreme after part of the ship between decks was called the gun room, a view of which may be seen in the introduction of this narrative in the description (plate 3). Here the officers among the prisoners had taken their place of abode, and from time and possession it had become as a room or separation from the sailors that they were entitled to, though they in reality had no pretensions to it, for their foes knew no distinction among us. We were rebels all. But they left us then to manage our concern in our own way.[18]

18. As "rebels," the Americans did not, in the British view, deserve the rights of prisoners of war, including recognition of rank and special treatment of officers. See pages xxiv–xxv.

As an officer (as I was) I found my way into this apartment called the gun room, where, with the rest of my late companions (officers), we were received with civility by the old occupants, who, though sorry to see us among them, upon the principle of humanity made us a tender of their services, and we were soon incorporated among them, and, having formed ourselves into messes according to our grade as much as possible, we became initiated into this family of human woes and partook of all their privations.

> Scarce had I mingled with this dismal band
> [A well known victim] seiz'd me by the hand–
> "And art thou come, (death heavy on his eyes)
> "And art thou come to these abodes," he cries.
> [Freneau]

In entering this hulk of a prison ship, it is necessary to get formed into a mess as soon as possible, but the first day of entrance will not admit of drawing anything of our allowance, and [on] the second, if we are enrolled, it will be too late to have it served out to us to have it cooked. No suffering from hunger reaches their ear, nor will they deviate from their usual hour of serving out upon any occasion, so that the poor, half-starved prisoner must absolutely wait until the second day before he can have anything boiled in the prisoners' copper. It was found to be best to get into some old, established mess (death daily making a vacancy in them). They are acquainted with the mode of procuring their pittance in time and avoid many impositions which a newcomer is liable to on his first introduction upon this stage of human woes.

Messing and Daily Allowance

[The messes] are all numbered and called in rotation, and at three o'clock the steward and his assistants attend at the window in the bulkhead of their room. At this time the prisoners

8th

Messing and daily Allowance

They are all Numbered and Call'd in Rotation, and at nine o'Clock the Steward, and his assistance attend at the window, in the Bulkhead of their room, at this time the Boatswain (that is one of the Mess) is ready in waiting, the Second of the Bell, lest they should not be in time on their Number being Called, to answer *here* — their Number being Call'd in Rotation, their allowance is handed out, very Expeditiously as I presume it is already prepared, previous to the time of Serving it out, the prisoner receives it for his Mess, be it what it will, in point of Quality, or Quantity, it will admit of no alteration when this, or any other Question — we as Prisoners, were only allow'd for Six Men — what they rated, an Allowance for four Men, it fell allowance, — that is, only two thirds, of what they allow their own Men in the Navy, which is at the rate here Mentioned —

″ Sunday 1st of August, one pound of Pork, & half a pint of Pease
″ Monday One pound of buisquit, and one pint of Oat meal & two ounces of Butter
″ Tuesday One pound of buisquit and two pounds of Beef
″ Wednesday One pound 8½ oz of flour, and two Ounces of Suit
″ Thursday the Same as on Sunday
″ Friday the Same as on Monday
″ Saturday the Same as Tuesday

hence from this allowance we, the prisoners, drew (if we had our due) two thirds of an allowance, of their own Men, as they Said — but it was of a very Inferior Quality, we Never Saw any Butter, but in lieu of it, they gave us (what they Call'd) Sweet Oil, but so rank and fetid that we could not Endure, even the Smell of it — we have an always took it and gave it away to the poor Half Starved french Men — who then received it very kindly, and with a little Salt, and their wormey bread, Seem'd to relish it very well, when I was on board the Fair Hope Prison Ship, in the year 1779 we had the Same Served out to us, there we used to burn it as we had the priviledge of light, until Nine o'Clock at night, — and it was usefull for that Purpose, but here we were allow'd no light, or fire, by night, on any Occasion whatever —

″ Such food they gave to make Compleat our woes,
″ it look'd like Carrion, torn from hungry Crows
″ your Meat or bread, thrown even of death supply
″ tis not our Care, to manage or provide
″ But this Base Relick dogs, I'd have you know,
″ that 'tis Better than you Merit, we bestow —

The narrative page for "Messing and Daily Allowance." (*Rhode Island Historical Society*) (that is one of [each] mess) is ready in waiting at the sound of the bell lest they should not be in time on their number being called to answer "here." Their number being called in rotation, their allowance is handed out very expeditiously, as I presume it is already prepared previous to the time of serving it out. The prisoner receives it for his mess. Be it what it will in point of quality or quantity, [they] will admit of no altercation upon this or any other occasion.

We as prisoners were allowed for six men what they rated an allowance for four men at full allowance, that is, only two thirds of what they allow their own men in the navy, which is at the rate here mentioned:

> Sunday: 1 pound of biscuit, 1 pound of pork, and 1/2 pint of peas
> Monday: 1 pound of biscuit, 1 pint of oatmeal, and 2 ounces of butter
> Tuesday: 1 pound of biscuit and 2 pounds of beef
> Wednesday: 1 1/2 pounds of flour and 2 ounces of suet
> Thursday: the same as on Sunday
> Friday: the same as on Monday
> Saturday: the same as on Tuesday[19]

19. It is difficult to tell from Dring whether this allowance applies to an individual or a mess, or, if an individual allowance, whether the *Jersey* prisoners received all or two-thirds of these amounts. Judging from Dring's further comments on page 35, this is the allowance for one person for one day in the British navy, where the messes were composed of four sailors each. Thus the *Jersey* prisoners, with their six-person messes, would each daily have received two-thirds of the amounts listed. In an affidavit quoted in the *New-York Gazette and Weekly Mercury*, February 12, 1781 (Onderdonk, *Revolutionary Incidents*, 235), Peter Robinson, acting purser on the *Jersey*, listed under oath the prisoner allowance, showing that at that time each prisoner received about the same amount of biscuit, more pork, less beef, and more butter than Dring reports, but no flour or suet.

Hence, from the allowance, we the prisoners drew (if we had our due) two-thirds of an allowance of their own men, as they said, but it was of a very inferior quality. We never saw any butter, but in lieu of it they gave us (what they called) sweet oil, but [it was] so rank and putrid that we could not endure even the smell of it. We, however, always took it and gave it away to the poor, half-starved Frenchmen who then received it very kindly and with a little salt and their wormy bread seemed to relish it very well.[20] When I was on board the *Good Hope* prison

20. Ebenezer Fox, another *Jersey* prisoner, from late 1780 to mid-1782, had some choice comments concerning the quality and quantity of food (*Adventures of Ebenezer Fox,* 102–5). For instance, on "pea day" he states, "I received the allowance of my mess, and behold! brown water and fifteen floating peas." Also, "the peas . . . were about as indigestible as grape shot." Concerning butter and biscuit, "had it not been for [the butter's] adhesive properties to retain together the particles of the biscuit that had been so riddled by the worms as to lose all their attraction of cohesion, we should have considered it no desirable addition to our viands." Alexander Coffin Jr., a prisoner on the *Jersey* late in 1782 and again in 1783, also penned some quotable comments in his letter to Dr. Samuel L. Mitchell, September 4, 1807, printed in Dawson's appendix, Dring-Greene, *Recollections,* 182. For example, concerning the pea soup, "And Sir, I might have defied any person on earth, possessing the most acute olfactory powers, and the most refined taste, to decide, either by one or the other, or both of those senses, whether it was pease [*sic*] and water, slush and water, or swill." All the prisoner narratives (see the sources listed in note 13 to the editor's introduction) agree that the provisions were abominable, both in quantity and quality. The provisions were mostly naval supplies of the same type fed to British sailors, but the prisoners suspected that they received old, spoiled provisions which the navy had discarded. British officials of course rejected that charge, and claimed that they fed the prisoners the best that could be had, given the fact that the British had no hinterland in America, from which to gather fresh supplies (see David Sproat to Abraham Skinner, January 29, 1781, quoted in the *New York Royal Gazette,* February 7, 1781, printed in Banks, *David Sproat,* 39–46). At other prisons, at New York and in England, the quantity of provisions was not greater. In fact isolated reports show that it was at times smaller. The

ship in the year 1779, we had the same [oil] served out to us. There we used to burn it, as we had the privilege of light until nine o'clock at night, and it was useful for that purpose. But here we were allowed no light or fire by night on any occasion whatever.[21]

> *Such food they sent, to make complete our woes,*
> *It look'd like carrion torn from hungry crows,*
> *//*
> *"Your meat or bread ([those men of death] replied)*
> *"Is not our care to manage or provide–*
> *"But this, damn'd rebel dogs, I'd have you know,*
> *"That better than you merit we bestow."*
> [Freneau]

Description of the Galley and Manner of Cooking

The cooking for the great mass of the prisoners on board the *Jersey* was done in the great copper, which would contain two or three hogsheads and sat in brickwork eight feet square under the forecastle, or what is commonly called the galley, a description of which will be seen in the introduction of this narrative, describing the hulk in plate 3.

Around this brickwork there had been driven from time to time by the prisoners spikes or hooks where they could suspend their tin kettles by the permission of our "sovereign cook" or his mates, of which I shall have occasion to speak hereafter. I shall here only give a description of the common boiler. It

quality was much superior, however, and especially in the English prisons, local fresh produce could be purchased by the prisoners, and at times was donated to them. See the sources listed in notes 13 and 16 of the editor's introduction.

21. This oil may have been what the prisoners used to burn the *Good Hope*, and this fire may explain why the *Jersey* prisoners were not allowed light at night (see note 11).

was composed of copper, and [from] using the sea water in boiling our victuals, from alongside, the copper became corroded and consequently poisonous, the fatal consequences of which must be obvious to everyone.

Having at length gotten our pittance, which frequently was not in time to have it boiled the same day, of course we had to wait until the next day unless we had a stack [of wood for fuel] on hand, or eat it raw, as necessity or our cravings stimulated. Having our pittance already prepared by being marked and numbered and awaiting the summons of the cook's bell, we thronged to the galley, and in few minutes hundreds of tallies [marked with different mess numbers] would be seen hanging over the sides of the brickwork by a line, watched by the owners, one of the mess being always in waiting to receive it when it was ready. The time the meat was in the boiler was always regulated by the time. Done or not done, the cook's bell was again the summons to receive it, to which we paid due attention. The delivery would admit no delay.

> *Ten minutes was the time he deign'd to stay,*
> *The time of grace allotted once a day–*
> [Freneau]

Our ship's cook was the only one that I could observe that had much flesh upon his bones, that is among them of long residence on board. He had been himself a prisoner among us, but finding no prospect of ever getting away, he had entered as ship's cook, and his mates and scullion were of the same stock. His plumpness could not possibly be the result of good living if he partook of the same quality of provisions as the rest of us. It is probable he drew more in quantity. I attribute it merely to a content of mind or a natural disposition to be so. He wore upon his head a greasy cap and really possessed a considerable share of good nature. He was often cursed by the prisoners (but not in his hearing) for his noncompliance with their requests, but taking into due consideration the great encumbrance we were to him around his "palace" and the many applications for some favor from him, I think he possessed an uncommon share of fortitude and forbearance, though to tell the truth, he did sometimes make the hot water fly amongst us, but a reconciliation soon took place again. His mates and scullion were not nearly so accommodating as their master.

I have before observed that around the brickwork in the galley there were hooks by which we were permitted to hang our tin kettles. As soon as we were allowed to come upon deck in the morning, one of the mess took the kettle up with him, having previously (the day before) provided some water for this purpose, and a few splinters of wood. We had soon taken possession of all the hooks around the brickwork, already to kindle a fire as soon as our sovereign cook would admit of it. To obtain a place was often a matter of contention among us but [was] decided by the cook or his mate, from which decision there was no appeal. Having procured fire, and the splinters of wood [being] duly applied under the kettle, we had only to watch it, and the moment it boiled, the brands (being ever so small) were quenched out and conveyed away for the next occasion. Another supplicant always stood ready to take the place and so on during the whole time there was fire allowed if the cook pleased to permit it. It required but very little wood to boil our kettle, the bottom of which was concave, [with] the splinters of wood applied directly at the center.

To procure water was another difficulty and was always procured the day beforehand little by little by each one composing the whole mess, as they would admit of only one pint to be taken away from the scuttle cask by the prisoners at one time by one person. It was therefore necessary that the whole mess should be employed in procuring it in time. But the mess to which I belonged always had some water in store as well as other necessaries, which we kept in a chest for that purpose.

During my stay of more than four months on board of the old *Jersey*, I never once partook of anyone thing that was cooked in the ship's copper.[22] It is to this circumstance that I (under divine Providence) attribute the maintenance of my health, and having it in my power to procure many necessary and comfortable things such as tea, sugar, etc., I was really in a better condition than most of my fellow sufferers in every respect, for which I desire to be very grateful.[23]

A Description [and some Observations]

It may be necessary just to mention that the copper boiler was square and had a partition in it in which the peas or oatmeal was boiled, for which purpose they allowed fresh water. They handed [it] out when boiled, in proportion to the quantity the prisoner put into the stack, which was their allowance of one day, say two-thirds of 1/2 pint each, twice a week, as before stated in our bill of fare. Methinks I can now see before me those miserable beings departing from the galley with their pittance of meat suspended from the string which had also

22. Dring's description of the cooking process is a bit confusing. Probably he actually did eat peas and oatmeal cooked in fresh water in the cooper. His and many other messes, however, chose not to boil their meat in the cooper. Instead they took turns making their own tiny fires at the brickwork, apparently when the cooper, with its large fire, was not in use. They undoubtedly were prohibited from lighting fires anywhere else in the ship for fear of the vessel's catching fire. Because of the desirability of private cooking, firewood became a coveted possession among the messes (see page 65).

23. In several additional instances Dring shows how much better a prisoner with money could live than one without. It appears that the officers, Dring included, did generally have some money to spend, but that most of the other prisoners had to subsist on whatever their captors gave them. Dring's comments on the subject reveal a sincere sensitivity concerning the lot of the ordinary seamen who were so much worse off than himself, limited, however, by a general acceptance of prevailing class differentiations.

accompanied it in the boiler, toddling away to the place of assemblage of the mess. There in tattered garments and death-like visages they view their only repast. With the remains of their wormy bread they divide this scanty morsel and devour it in a moment. Thus day after day the emaciated prisoner drags along his fainting body with one continual craving, the effects of an empty stomach. No kinds of vegetable whatever are afforded by our inhuman keepers, nor has the prisoner the means to procure it.[24] Good God, what a luxury would it have been to them to have only a few potatoes, the very leavings of the swine of our country.

I have before mentioned that we occupied two decks, one above the other. I used to observe great numbers passing, that is, ascending and descending the stairs which led to the lower hold, but I never had the disposition to visit this place of appar-ent wretchedness, but it did [seem], if I may judge from the appearance of the occupants, to be a more dismal place of abode than that where I resided. They appeared to be princi-pally foreigners or some who had survived every malady to which the human frame is subjected, [having] scarcely tatters sufficient to cover their nakedness, long beards, and dirty faces.[25] It may be asked, "Why did they neglect their person,

24. It is not clear why vegetables were not available from the bumboat for those who could pay (see pages 61–63). Also see note 41 concerning the pos-sibility that the prisoners had direct access to vegetables and other food on shore.

25. The foreigners on prison ships at New York (mostly French and Spanish) appear from this and other narratives to have been treated by both their cap-tors and some American prisoners worse than the Americans were treated by the British. Interestingly enough, the opposite was apparently true in the English prisons, to the point that it became an issue of heated debate in Parliament, fired by humanitarians and friends of the American rebellion. See *Adventures of Ebenezer Fox*, 107–8; *Memoranda* by Roswell Palmer, quoted in Dawson's appendix, Dring-Greene, *Recollections*, 179; passage from the British

why not wash and shave themselves or mend their garments?",
but they had not the means. Their clothes, probably all they
had when they entered this hulk, were upon their backs. They
were now entirely worn out. They had nothing to patch them
with, not even thread or needle to work with nor the means to
procure it. They had no soap or razor to shave with, and the
beard was only occasionally reduced by a pair of shears or scis-
sors which was done by another person and left their faces in
a frightful condition. Their shirts could only be stamped out
upon the deck with their feet in salt water and their bodies
naked during the operation. Their skin, by continual washing
in salt water, had become corroded, nor had they the means to
appear cleanly, but, after all, much undoubtedly originated
from neglect which had become habitual, and a total indifference as to appearance had possessed them.[26]

"'But,' you will ask, 'was there no relief for these victims of
misery?'–No–their astonishing sufferings were concealed from
the view of the world–and it was only from the few witnesses
of the scene who afterwards lived to tell the cruelties they
endured, that our country became acquainted with their
deplorable condition. The grim sentinels, faithful to their
charge as fiends of the nether world, barred the doors against
the hand of charity, and godlike benevolence never entered
there–compassion had fled from these mansions of despair,
and pity wept over other woes.

"'But', you will ask again, 'was there no means of escape
from these habitations of distress?'–No–there was no escape,
except in death, or in that which, to freemen, was worse than

---

Annual Register for 1781, 152, quoted in Jeremiah Johnson's *Recollections of
Brooklyn and New York*, printed in Dawson's appendix, 192.

26. In contrast to this, prisoners in the English prisons were given soap from
time to time and had a pump in the prison yard for washing themselves and
their clothes. See, for example, Herbert, *Relic of the Revolution*, 85; Coan,
"Revolutionary Prison Diary," 302.

death–the service of the enemy. Few could ever gain their liberty by being exchanged;" and few, to [their] immortal honor,
of those suffering men, ever entered the service of the enemy.
I never knew a solitary instance of it during my captivity on
board of two prison ships.[27] "This indeed was the chief glory of
these martyrs of liberty, that no rewards nor punishments
could move them to betray their country. Firm in their purpose, as the everlasting hills . . . was there no source of consolation, no ray of comfort in the midst of all their suffering . . . ?

27. Dring himself has much to say about guard cruelty (especially on pages
75–81), escape possibilities (84–92), and exchange possibilities (92–98). His
repetition of De Witt's oratory about the fortitude of prisoners who preferred
death to joining the British service clouds the fact that many in fact did join
the British navy, a few at least with the express purpose of subsequently
escaping (see pages xx and xxviii to the editor's introduction); *Adventures of
Ebenezer Fox*, 147–49. The number of prisoner desertions worried American
military officials. See, for instance, Abraham Skinner to General Washington
on December 24, 1871 (Banks, *David Sproat*, 63); Washington to the
Continental Congress on December 27, 1781 (ibid., 60); Secretary of War
Benjamin Lincoln to the President of Congress, June 28, 1782 (ibid., 99).
Some prisoners attempted to attract relief by writing letters and petitions to
local newspaper editors threatening to join the British if relief was not quickly forthcoming. See, for example, a letter from a *Jersey* prisoner dated August
10, 1781, quoted in the *Philadelphia Pennsylvania Packet*, September 4, 1781,
printed in Bushnell's notes to *Adventures of Christopher Hawkins*, 261; printed
on the same page of Bushnell's notes, a letter dated April 26, 1782, quoted in
the *Philadelphia Pennsylvania Packet*, May 21, 1782; a letter from six *Jersey*
prisoners dated June 11, 1782, quoted in the *New-York Gazette and Weekly
Mercury*, June 17, 1782, printed in Dawson's appendix, Dring-Greene,
Recollections, 142. Suffering of the degree experienced on the *Jersey* was not
the only inducement to desertion of the cause, for in three months in late
1778 and early 1779, forty-nine of about three hundred American prisoners in
Old Mill Prison, Plymouth, England, were pardoned by the king and joined
the British forces (see Herbert, *Relic of the Revolution*, 171, 215). This included an unusual group enlistment of thirty-three men. Still, enlistments from
the English prisons were regular occurrences. See the sources listed in note
19 to the editor's introduction.

Yes . . . [we] felt [a consolation that] the slave never feels, and which the inexorable vengeance of tyrants can never destroy–the *love* of country, and the *hope* of immortality: these supported [us through our] agonies, and raised them superior to the ills of life–without these [our] prison had been in very deed a hell . . . . As for these mortal bodies, and these immortal spirits,–'O God! O God!–there is another and a better world!'" [De Witt, 87–91].

To observe with what persevering fortitude the sufferers bore up under all their privations is almost incredible, and scarcely anything short of being an eye witness to the scene itself could have established it in my firm belief. But alas, the picture is not too highly colored. I know from experience it is founded in facts. I witnessed the fatal and "lingering torments of a doleful prison [ship where we were] wasted away by corroding grief, [our] vitals torn by the perpetual gnawing of hunger, consumed by burning thirst devoured piece-meal by famine [and] pestilence . . . . And yet it shook not the fortitude of the American prisoner" [De Witt, 91].

> *Americans! a just resentment shew,*
> *And glut revenge on this detested foe;*
> *While the warm blood exults the glowing vein*
> *Still shall resentment in our bosoms reign.*
> [Freneau]

The Working Party

It had been a long established custom on board the *Jersey* to have what was there called the working party. [This] consisted of about twenty able-bodied men from among the prisoners, and one of the officers of the same class took his turn daily to preside over them. The men were stationary and headed by what they called the boatswain, and they received a compensation for their labor. Their duty was to wash down the deck and gangway throughout that part of the ship where the prisoners resorted, to spread the awning (after we had one), and to hoist in the water from the craft that brought it alongside, as also the wood or whatever else was to be taken on board in the course of the day. And after the prisoners were permitted to ascend upon deck at 8 o'clock with all their movables (if it was a fair day) consisting of all hammocks and all bedding, for the purpose of washing out between decks, their things were then all placed upon the booms (or spar deck so called). This party together with the nurses removed the disabled to the bunks and the dead upon the deck, after which a general washing took place between decks. The prisoners were generally kept on deck during this operation unless it was such as were disposed to assist in the performance of this business, and the beds and clothing were kept on deck until near the time we were to be driven below for the night. During this interval, when all the chests had been piled up and every hammock [was] on deck [and] the deck washed and swabbed up dry, it was quite a luxury to walk under deck free from all its encumbrances except that of the sick in their bunks. The air seemed to circulate through our breathing places, and we promenaded the spacious room with some pleasure for a short duration of a few hours.

> But they no groves nor grassy mountains tread,
> Mark'd for a longer journey to the dead.
> [Freneau]

We had several large tubs which were placed around the railing leading to the hatchway of the lower deck (as described in the drawing number 3 in the introduction). Those were emptied by the working party before mentioned in the morning and remained on deck during the day. At about 4 o'clock in the afternoon we were ordered to down hammocks etc. This was a busy time among us [with] such a multitude all in motion at the same time.

Swift from the guarded decks we rush'd along,
And vainly sought repose, so vast our throng.
[Freneau]

Our Situation [and a Few Observations]

From the time we were directed to take our things below, say from 4 o'clock until the setting sun, was an interval of two hours.[28] During this time we were permitted to remain on deck or stay below, as we pleased. It was really the most pleasant part of the twenty-four hours, if any pleasantness could be discerned among us. We had gotten through another day. Our washing, scrubbing, and [de]lousing had been done, and we devoted the remaining hour to the luxury of our evening pipe. Short indeed was the space of this interval. We were soon ordered to descend to our gloomy and dreadful abode for the night. The working party was directed to put the tubs below, which accomplished, they descended themselves. The gratings laid, the sentinel having taken his place, we were left to pass another dismal night, [as] too feebly already described, with the heinous sentinel from above singing aloud through the night, "All's well."

The tubs above alluded to were for the use of the prisoners by night or such time as we were confined below, and although they were absolutely necessary in our confined condition, they [were] very offensive, and it was with difficulty they could be reached by those who had occasion to visit them in utter darkness, particularly as we had to tread over many who were strewn along upon the deck to sleep, though all had avoided, as far as in their power, a place of repose near those tubs, both on account of their smell and the liability of being

28. From 4:00 p.m. to sunset at New York during the summer is actually closer to four hours.

often trod upon or disturbed in the night. Yet all could not avoid this ill convenience, as all could not get within the limits made use of as a sleeping place, [as] described in the introduction in plate 3.

> *Some for a bed their tatter'd vestments join,*
> *And some on chests, and some on floors recline.*
> [Freneau]

It was customary among the prisoners to get as near the ship's side as possible to sleep and also to have a breathing place through the iron gratings in the side of the ship. It not only secured us from being trod upon by night but also afforded a breathing place, which was very desirable, particularly by night when the nauseous smell was scarcely to be endured. It also afforded us a place to empty our water etc. out of [the ship]. I had such a situation during my stay on board the *Jersey*. Our chests or boxes were placed about ten feet from the ship's side with the lock inward, a partition of the same by ourselves and our next neighbors thus affording an enclosure of about ten feet where the mess assembled and slept, one, however, upon the chest by way of security. Thus arranged, as much room was left in the middle as our crowded situation would admit of, though considerably encumbered with hammocks by night.

We were generally ordered below at sunset, as before mentioned, and having gotten near to our enclosure or sleeping place, here [we passed] a dreary night in utter darkness. But silence was a stranger to us. There was a continual noise during the night proceeding from various causes, some the effects of pain and some from delirium but mostly the effects of heat or suffocation and the curses copiously bestowed upon our merciless foe, to whom we very justly attributed all our sufferings by being cooped up in so narrow and limited space when they had it so abundantly in their power to extend our limit and give a space to breathe in.

This scene of one night may serve to only show what we experienced generally, but there were exceptions when our sufferings were augmented and the consequences fatal. Notwithstanding all the numerous maladies that we were subjected to on board the *Jersey*, I have known many who it was said had been two years on board and were apparently very well. They had undoubtedly gone through the furnace and become what they call seasoned. They had given up all idea of ever being exchanged and were mostly foreigners and appeared not to have that hankering after home as we from the northward had. Indeed, they appeared to be lost to society and quite indifferent as to their place of abode.

> *Meagre and wan, and scorch'd with heat below,*
> *[They] loom'd like ghosts, ere death had made [them] so*
> [Freneau]

On the contrary, the prisoners from the northern states, which were the most numerous among us, were mostly young men and raw hands whose necessity or inclination had induced them to go to sea. They were generally taken almost as soon as they reached the ocean, and the sudden change to them was almost death, and more particularly, after they had reached the abode of the old *Jersey*, the dismal objects with which they were now surrounded, in most instances deprived of their wearing apparel by their captors, the vermin with which they became infested, their now scanty and miserable diet, together with the hankering after their homes and the sight of their dearest connections and friends whom they left only a short time before, this combination of circumstances had a wonderful effect upon this class of people, and dejection was visible upon their countenances. It produced dismay, and they absolutely, many of them, died with grief or a broken heart.[29]

29. This emotional conclusion contrasts somewhat with Dring's and De Witt's previous observations (pages 37–38), equally emotional, about the

Deny'd the comforts of a dying bed,
And not a pillow to support the head–
How could they else but pine, and grieve, and sigh,
Detest a wretched life–and wish to die?
[Freneau]

A Short Description of the *Jersey*

A view of this hulk may be seen in the drawings numbered 1., 2., and 3. in the first part of this narrative [see pages 10–15], but in order to give the reader a better idea of our situation, I have thought proper to give a further description of her. The quarterdeck ran about one-fourth part over what was called the upper deck, and the forecastle ran [over] about one-eighth part from forward. From the quarterdeck to the forecastle was a gangway about five feet wide by which we were allowed to pass and repass. On this gangway the sentinels were placed on each side. The intermediate space over this deck, that is from the bulkhead of the quarterdeck to the forecastle, was filled up with long spars or booms and was called the spar deck.

This temporary deck was very useful to the prisoners. It was here that our movables were placed while the between decks was under the operation of cleaning out, which was every fair day. It also served to keep off the scorching rays of the sun and sometimes the rain and was the only place we had to walk in and was continually occupied by us for this purpose in whole battalions, all walking one way and turning at the same time. On the starboard side was the derrick and on the larboard side the accommodation ladder, descending from the gangway down to the water, at the head of which also stood a sentinel. This place was near to the door of the barricade. The barricade was ten feet high and projected a few feet over the sides.

prisoners' fortitude and endurance in the face of extreme suffering, even with the temptation to join the British service for relief.

Through this were loopholes made through which they might fire upon us if necessity should require.

> *At every post some surly vagrant stands,*
> *Pick'd from the [English] or the [Scottish] bands.*
> [Freneau]

The ship's crew was composed of a captain, two mates, steward, cook, and about twelve sailors.[30] Their accommodation ladder was upon the other side of the ship and led up nearby the after part of the ship, having no communication with the prisoners whatever. No prisoner was ever permitted to pass through the barricade door except when it was necessary to have the messes examined and regulated. In this case we had everyone of us to pass through and down between decks under a guard of soldiers and there remain until this operation had been gone through with. Nor did the guard or any part of the ship's crew ever come among the prisoners. During the whole time that I was on board the Jersey, I saw an officer or man that belonged to her only as they passed in their boat to the stern ladder etc. The forward part of the ship upon the same deck was the galley, as before mentioned and described in Plate 3., as also [are] the other apartments.

The Hospital Ships

We had, during the summer of seventeen hundred and eighty-two, at the time I was on board the *Jersey* prison ship, upon an average of about one thousand prisoners (exclusive of the sick on board the hospital ships),[31] composed of all people whom

30. Compare this list with the expanded one on page 117.

31. Estimates of the number of prisoners on the *Jersey* vary from under 400 to more than 1,200 in different narratives at different times. The trend, however, was toward greater numbers and more crowded conditions, so that by the middle of 1782 the 1,000 figure appears to be fairly accurate, if not low. The official American estimate in the summer of 1782 was 800, but that num-

the English were at that time at war, but the principal part was taken in American vessels, and this hulk was a depot for sailors only. I never knew any soldier to be put on board of her. That class of prisoners, if any, was confined in what they called the Sugar House or Provost at New York.[32] I mention this circumstance that the reader may know whom the prisoners were composed of and the distinction between sailors and soldiers at that time.

The *Jersey* [was] becoming so crowded and the mortality on board every day was increasing [so much] by fever and other maladies that the hospital ships to which they had been removed were scarcely roomy [enough] for their reception. Under this dreadful circumstance, a part of the upper deck of the *Jersey* had been converted to the use of the sick, and bunks were provided and there placed on the after part of the larboard side where those who felt the symptoms of approaching sickness would lay themselves down, to be found by the nurses as soon as possible. It served also as a place of security from

ber probably excludes the foreign prisoners. See Abraham Skinner to David Sproat, June 24, 1782, printed in Banks, *David Sproat*, 90. By way of contrast, in each of the two English prisons the numbers seem to have varied from about 175 to 350 Americans, averaging about 275. French, Spanish, and Dutch prisoners lived separately. Although the total prisoner population in each prison averaged nearly 1,000, each nationality group seems to have had its own dormitory and courtyard. See *Memoirs of Andrew Sherburne*, 83–85, and the sources listed in note 19 to the editor's introduction.

32. Conditions in these prisons were cause for much complaint among their inmates. These were, however, better places to live than the prison ships. The Provost was a VIP prison where, among others, a few privateer captains were held, including Silas Talbot. A major complaint there was directed against the insulting and cruel manner of the Provost Marshall, Captain William Cunningham. After the war, the British seem to have caught him embezzling government funds, for which he is said to have been hanged in England in 1791 (see Onderdonk, *Revolutionary Incidents*, 207–10, 245–47; Dandridge, *American Prisoners*, 33–47. See also the sources listed in note 16 to the editor's introduction.

being otherwise trod or trampled upon, to which they were liable while lying on the deck.

> *From morn to eve along the decks we lay*
> *Scorch'd into fevers by the solar ray.*
> [Freneau]

They had also three hospital ships moored near the old *Jersey*, namely the *Scorpion*, the *Strombolo*, and the *Hunter*, one of which, however, was more of a store ship and a depot of medical apparatus and a station for the doctor's mates and the boat's crew attending the whole. But as I have never been on board [any] of them, I can only give a faint description of them, and but very few ever returned from them that I know of [so] that I could never learn their treatment on board of them. I can only judge from the dreadful appearances of them, viewed from the *Jersey*. They were of a forbidding and disgusting nature, and sickening to the imagination. Knowing as we did who their tenants were composed of, we felt a dread now steal upon us, thinking we might soon be an inmate of those abodes truly of wretchedness which, viewed from our station, had a more terrifying appearance than even our own hulk whose appearance we could then not observe from the interior where we were. To [the sick], however, the change might be considered for the better in some respects if not all.[33]

33. See Bushnell's notes to *Adventures of Christopher Hawkins*, 238–43, for background information on the three hospital ships. Other narratives containing further information about hospital ship life show that conditions were about as Dring suspected. Medical care was infrequent and primitive, and in winter there was no heat, and snow filtered through the seams. Although there were bunks, prisoners were at times crowded two to a bunk, and food and water were not much better than on the *Jersey*. See especially *Memoirs of Andrew Sherburne*, 112–16. The incidence of disease (mostly yellow fever, dysentery, and smallpox) on the prison ships was colossal in comparison with the prisons in England. Of course there was sickness there also, and

There no soft voice their bitter fate bemoan'd,
And Death strode stately, while the victims groan'd.
[Freneau]

Signals

As I have before mentioned, one of those called [a] hospital ship was a kind of depot for the medical department (I think it was the *Hunter*). I recollect of once having seen a coffin brought from her to the *Jersey*. It was for Captain Brooks who died shortly after being on board. He was a remarkably stout and robust man. Such men generally were the greatest victims to the prevailing fever. A day or two terminated their existence. As bad as these hideous hulks appeared to us, they were undoubtedly far preferable to that of the *Jersey*. There they had no well men to contend with and more room to breathe in. They had also the benefit of an awning and a wind sail [attached] to each hatchway to conduct the fresh air down between decks where the sick lay, and the hatchway was left open by night, as our kind keepers were under little or no apprehension from this class of feeble victims in their present condition.

When anything was wanted, it was made known by the different ships by signal and was promptly attended to by the boat or boats from the *Hunter*. We soon learned the signal to convey away the dead from the ships to the bluff. It was a yellow whiff at the ensign staff. Our condition made great work for those who presided over us, and their employment, I presume, was not altogether to some of them agreeable. Very few ever returned from the hospitals to the *Jersey*. I recollect only

some of it was smallpox, but the few infected were quickly removed to hospitals, where apparently many recovered to return to the main prison. A prevalent though less serious malady in the English prisons was called "the itch." See the sources listed in note 19 to the editor's introduction.

two or three solitary instances while I was on board of her, and
those met with the following greeting on their return.

> *"Why didst thou leave the* Scorpion's *dark retreat,*
> *"And hither hast a surer death to meet?*
> *"[Even if thou had a] damp infected cell,*
> *"If that was purgatory, this is hell—"*
> [Freneau]

We had on board the *Jersey* about half a dozen men who were
called nurses. They were of the prisoners, and I never learned
by whom they were appointed. Perhaps they were self-created.
I only know that they were all thieves. They might, however,
in some cases be useful so far as to assist the sick from between
decks up to the gangway, there to be examined by the visiting
doctor who came daily from the *Hunter* for the purpose (if the
weather was good), and if they were deemed a proper candidate for the hospital ship, they were gotten into the boat in
waiting, not, however, without the loss or detention of all their
effects (if they had any), as I have before mentioned.

One instance I shall mention which may serve to show the
treatment of the whole of those poor, fainting, dying mortals
left to [the nurses'] care and about to be transported to the
hospital ship and probably soon to the bank.

Nurses

Mr. Robert Carver (our gunner on board the *Chance*) was taken
sick. I found him in one of the bunks on that side of the ship
where they crawled to when they had a desire to be removed,
as before mentioned. He had neither bed nor pillow but had
on all the wearing apparel he possessed, which I presume was
by way of precaution to save it (knowing his condition). The
weather was extremely warm, and where he then lay [it] was
almost sufficient to suffocate him. He had on his great coat at
the same time.

I found him sitting up on end in the bunk and feeling in his hat, which he had between his knees, for some needles which he said his wife had sent him.[34] I at once discovered that a delirium had then taken place on him, [which] was a sure presage to an approaching end. I got his great coat off and placed [it] under his head for a pillow and laid him down while I went away to procure him some tea and was only a few minutes then absent from him.

On my return I met one of those thieves called a nurse with his great coat and challenged it. He said that it was a perquisite of the nurses and the only one that they had and that the man was dying and the garment could be of no further use to him. I, however, took it away from him, [it] being a pretty good one, that is for the times (and brought it home to his family).

Mr. Carver soon expired in the clothes he had on. We, however, procured a blanket for his corpse, and he was as decently buried as any of his companions under the bluff. This was the first opportunity that I had to go onshore, upon this occasion. He, however, was not the first victim of our crew. He was a man of robust constitution. To such the fever was violent, and death soon relieved them.

I have no blame to attach to our foe as regards the thieving disposition of the nurses over whom they could have no control, and only mention the circumstance of Mr. Carver's treatment to show to what a state of wretchedness we were now reduced (sick or well). Mr. Carver was well known by many hundreds who are now living in Providence, where dwell some of his posterity at this, the time of my writing. If I have been particular in this case, it was only to avoid a repetition, as it may serve to give some idea to the reader of the whole. The mode of interment I shall speak of in the next page from my

34. The manuscript is unclear here. The word could be "needles" or "nudles" (noodles), either of which would preserve the sense of the description.

own personal attendance upon several occasions while I was on board of the *Jersey* prison ship.

> *In barren sands, and far from home, they lie,*
> *No friend to shed a tear, when passing by;*
> *O'er the mean tombs insulting Britons tread,*
> *Spurn at the sand, and curse the rebel dead.*
> [Freneau]

Burial of the Dead [and some Reflections]

When the between decks was examined for the sick and the dead, the sick were placed in the bunks, as before stated, and the corpses were carried upon deck and laid upon the gratings. If [there was] anyone who was disposed to sew them up in a blanket, if they could procure one for them, they were permitted to do it. They had a board strapped with rope on which the corpses were laid, because they might be yet too warm or not stiff enough to send into the boat by a single strap. The corpse was let into the boat then in waiting, the signal being previously given for the boat to come from the *Hunter* for this purpose, and if any dead were taken from on board the hospital ships on their way to the *Jersey*, they were in the boat. The tackle was applied, and the corpses were let into the boat, one at a time by way of decency.

The prisoners were always gasping to get permission to go into the boat upon this occasion, not so much upon the principle of humanity (to which they had become strangers) as respected one another, but merely to have the satisfaction of once more putting their feet upon their native soil. The number allowed being pointed out, they descended into the boat with the guard of soldiers with them and put off from the ship for the shore. There was a short wharf where we landed near which was a hut containing the handbarrows and shovels. Having placed the corpses on those handbarrows, they were conveyed to the side of the bank at the Wallabout before described. Some with shovels and some with hoes, we proceeded on with our fellow sufferers who had paid the [debt] of nature, and when suitable place or vacancy was found, we were directed to dig a trench according to the length then required for the number of victims. We dug on until we were directed to stop, it being deep enough in their opinion. The corpses were there deposited and the sand hauled down over them, which we had scarcely time to accomplish without any more ceremony, and the transaction had no more effect upon our guard than if they had buried any common animal, and the word was given to march, scarcely giving us time to look around, but [it] was sufficient to show us many bodies exposed partly to view, who probably had been only a few days [before] lowered in like manner.

> *Despensing death triumphantly they stand,*
> *Their musquets ready to obey command;*
> //
> *By feeble hands the shallow graves were made,*
> *No stone memorial o'er the corpses laid;*
> //
> *And o'er the tombs, if tombs can then be found,*
> *Place the green turf, and plant the myrtle round.*
> [Freneau]

After having performed this last duty of burying as well as our enemies would permit us to do, we reluctantly retraced our steps toward the boats with the guard on each side of us. A return to our pestilential confinement was truly distressing to us, particularly as we had experienced on this occasion the exquisite pleasure of breathing the sweet air of our native soil. As we had to pass by the water side, we implored permission of our guards to permit us to bathe or wash ourselves for a moment, but it would not be complied with.

I believe I was the only one among the prisoners who had at this time a pair of shoes on. I well recollect the circumstance of my taking them off my feet that I might have the pleasure of feeling the earth, or rather the sand, into which we shoved our feet along. And when we reached a spot where there was some sod, we tore up pieces of it and by permission were allowed to take it on board for our comrades to smell of. It was sought after by them with assiduity and passed around like a fragrant rose among them. To those who never experienced the want of a soil to tread upon or the sweet and circulating air to breathe may think the above a trifling subject to thus dwell upon, but permit me to assure all such that had they been placed there in the situation that we were at that time and place, it would have produced the same effect upon them, which, however, I hope they may never experience.

As I passed sadly along with the dreary thought of again entering that most odious hulk and [thinking] that a few minutes longer and we must be obliged to quit our own native soil probably for the last time while alive, I here reflected upon the manner we had deposited our fellow prisoners and that some of us who had then assisted perhaps would shortly be placed by their side, and in the same manner, [with] not even a sod to cover the grave if grave it could be called. I could not but think that "the great man who . . . dies in the days of tranquility and peace, [has] his name enrolled on the page of history, and his virtues inscribed in the temple of religion", while the victims in their country's cause have not even a sod to cover them or a stone to point out their resting place. But "shall not their . . . virtues be told to posterity" even if their names are not known? It is from this motive that I now undertake to give this feeble description of a funeral for a poor victim who sank "under the [accumulated sufferings] of a vindictive foe" [De Witt, 84].

> *In sickly hulks, devoted while we lay,*
> *Successive funerals gloom'd each dismal day–*

//
Each day, at least [six] carcasses we bore,
And scratch'd them graves along the sandy shore.
[Freneau]

We had retraced our steps back to the boat, having deposited the handbarrows, shovels, etc. into the hut before mentioned, there to rest until the next day when probably they would be used for the same sad purpose. We were indulged with the delayance of nearly half an hour upon the landing place. Be it now remembered that our guard at this time were Hessians to whom we were indebted for this respite for a short time.

While here, we turned our eyes from the disgusting old *Jersey* and her satellites (the hospital ships) and directed them toward the abode of a mansion, the habitation of a miller [named Remsen]. It was told us that there was near the house a tide mill [and] that the short wharf where we now were was for the convening of the same. Oh, how I wished to enter this dwelling where probably dwelt harmony and peace and the white walls that in our more happy moments we had been accustomed to. This house generally went by the name of "the Dutchman's house." It was venerated by the prisoners on account of its being the residence of his amiable daughter who, it was said, had always kept a regular account of the number of victims landed at this wharf for interment from the *Jersey* and the hospital ships.[35] We, however, saw nothing of her or anyone else upon this occasion. It was not necessary to approach the boat for this purpose [of counting victims], as it could be well ascertained from the windows of the house, nor would it be then deemed prudent to approach us, moving bodies of pestilence and filth.

We had only four to bury on this occasion. One of the party then observed that the good girl had not quite a tally [i.e. a full

35. There is no extant record of such an account.

mess of six men]. It was astonishing to hear the remarks of those inconsiderate sailors. One would observe, "It may be my turn next, Jack! Give us a good covering if you can, that is. Haul a plenty of sand over me." etc.

We were now bidden to enter the boat, and sadly approaching the hulk, we ascended the ladder and descended the hatchway to our former place of wretched abode conveying, each one, a piece of sod to our companions as a nosegay which was duly received and properly appreciated by the prisoners.

Permit me here to remark that many of us then in confinement had been accustomed to be long on shipboard while at sea, but it was then upon the ocean where the air is sweet and wholesome [with] no sight of land to excite our desires. But here, [being] only a few rods off the shore, not in a foreign country but [in] the land of our nativity, where we could see the fruitful trees and the luxuriant meadows with numerous herds of cattle feasting upon the productions, only served to convince us of the tantalizing object of our foes in thus placing us where we even envied the condition of the cattle.[36]

Death Begins to Make Inroads Among our Crew

Having now returned to my confinement, the scene and every direful object around me appeared more disgusting, if possible, than it had ever before done. Several weeks had now elapsed since my entrance into those dark, infernal abodes, and I had in some measure become familiarized unto the scene. But a short visit on shore had a tendency to make me feel all my wretchedness and view my situation with abhorrence and despair.

---

36. Dring is here alluding to the supposed policy of the British to make imprisonment as unbearable as possible, to induce prisoners to join the British service for relief of their sufferings.

I have before observed that this was the first time that I had been permitted to go on shore, though Mr. Carver, whose burial I had then attended, was not the first victim of our crew. The first was the youngest, a lad of about twelve years of age by the name of Palmer. While on board the *Chance*, this boy attended upon the officers, and after we got on board the *Jersey* he continued in the same capacity and made one of the number of the mess to which I then belonged. He had, with many others, been inoculated for the small pox immediately after entering the *Jersey*. It did not appear to take well. He, however, at the usual time broke out very full. Appearances were very favorable, the pock full, and we supposed him to be doing well. But all at once it flattened in and a yellow countenance bespoke at once, the fatal approach of death. Delirium soon took place and that night terminated his existence.

It was truly heart-piercing to me to hear the screeches of this amiable boy calling in his delirium for the assistance of his mother and others I suppose composing a part of his family. This night was truly a painful one to me, most of which was spent in holding him in his convulsed state, and that in utter darkness. Arguments on any persuasion to silence his groans and supplications were useless, but exhausted nature, however, soon did its office. His screams became less piercing and his strength more feeble. I could not see him die in our midnight gloom, but I found by placing my hand near his mouth when he ceased to breathe and when the last breath quit his mortal frame.

Returning light presented his lovely [*sic*] corpse to my sad view. I was truly affected by this occurrence. The lad had always looked up to me as a protector, particularly during his sickness, but I had done all that my limited condition would then admit of. I had only to assist in sewing the corpse up in a blanket, and he was at the usual hour conveyed on deck among others and at the hour of interment was conveyed into the boat in the manner already described, and his late actual limbs were committed to the trench under the bank and covered with sand.

I very much regretted that I could not attend at his funeral, but my health would not admit of it, being then just broken out with the small pox, nor do I know if I could have obtained permission if I had asked it. They had no idea that we could have any sympathy for each other, but supposed we were as cold-hearted as themselves. I will here only observe that if there was any such thing as sympathy among them it was only among the Hessians. Indeed, the prisoners themselves had lost their humanity toward each other, not having it in their power to render assistance to each other. They had become callous, and self preservation was their only study.

The next victim of our crew (that came to my knowledge) was that of James Mitchell. He was the oldest man among the crew of the *Chance* and was well known among the citizens of Providence within the recollections of many at the present time of my writing, for most all knew Jimmy Mitchell, and what is something extraordinary, Thomas Sturmey, his son-in-law, died at the same time. I did not know that they were even sick, and their death was communicated to me while their corpses were upon the grating in the clothes they died in. We, however, procured them blankets to be sewed up in, and they were conveyed on shore and buried in the manner as heretofore mentioned. I sought to get permission to attend at this funeral but could not obtain liberty to do it. I, however, watched their progress with my eyes from the hulk and saw them deposited under the bank, the result of which, among others, will be hereafter fully described, [how] their precious bones were all collected and, after a lapse of twenty-five years, were reburied or met sepultral rites, as I shall again mention in its proper place at the close of this narrative.[37]

37. See page 124 and note 5.

I mentioned that I knew not of the sickness of those my companions in captivity, and [though] fellow townsmen, it must be observed that we were not placed near each other on board. We sometimes met each other among the multitude and inquiry was made as to the fate of our old comrades, from which inquiry I have heard of [the] death of some of our former crew, which never came to my knowledge at the time it took place, and others had been removed to the hospital ships, to which I was not acquainted. In short, we were a little wretched world within the walls of putrefaction and obscurity, surrounded by the languid and the dead.

> *"Thus do our warriers, thus our heroes fall,*
> *"Imprison'd here, base ruin meets them all,"*
> //
> *"Ah! rest in peace, poor, injur'd parted shade,*
> *"By cruel hands in death's dark weeds array'd."*
> [Freneau]

The Guards

I have stated that the ship's crew consisted of a captain, two mates, boatswain, steward, and about twelve sailors, and about a dozen old and invalided marines who were stationary on board the ship. The other guard was composed of soldiers from the regiments quartered upon Long Island, and their number at the time of duty [was] maybe about thirty, and [they were] relieved once a week, that is by English, Hessians, and refugees. We prisoners always preferred the Hessians.[38]

38. This interesting point of view, which Dring expresses several times, may reflect the Hessians' lesser emotional involvement in the issues of the conflict, in contrast to the highly charged mutual hostility between American revolutionaries and loyalists. The prevalent attitude within the Continental army seems to have been somewhat different. To them the Hessians were merciless, unfeeling mercenaries, to be despised for having sold themselves to the forces of tyranny.

They were considered more accommodating to us, though we had no complaints from the English. They only obeyed their instructions as respected us.

But the refugees or royalists, as they affected to call themselves, were the most obnoxious to us. I, however, do not recollect of having those miscreants placed over us more than three times, and the whole of that time was attended with tumult. The prisoners could not abide the sight of them and gave them occasionally abusive language. They in their turn treated us with all the severity in their power. We dared not approach near them for fear of the bayonet. We could not pass by the gangway as usual when they on sentry walked but were obliged to crawl upon the booms to get fore and aft or up and down to the hatchways. They never made any reply to our remarks about them but would point to their clothing as much as to say, "We are clothed by our sovereign, while you are naked." I know they were always as glad to get rid of us as we were to be rid of them. Our curses generally followed them when they left us as far as they could hear us, [along with] many provoking gestures, which was all we could do, and it was bestowed upon them copiously by the prisoners.

There was then a regiment of those refugees quartered at Brooklyn. Their uniform was green. We were invited to join this royal band and to partake of his majesty's pardon and bounty, but the prisoners spurned at their proffered offer, and although "their sufferings and their sorrows were great, [yet] unbounded was their fortitude. Under every privation and every anguish of life, they firmly encountered the terrors of death, rather than desert the cause of their country" [De Witt, 86], and I never knew one single instance of enlistment under their banners while I was with them.

> *Ah! traitors, lost to every sense of shame,*
> *Unjust supporters of a tyrant's claim;*
> *Foes to the rights of freedom and of men,*

Flush'd with the blood of thousands you have slain,
To the just doom the righteous skies decree
We leave you, toiling still in cruelty.
[Freneau]

The only duty that I observed done by those old marines was to guard the water butt, near which scuttle cask one took his station with a drawn cutlass. Their orders, it seems, were to let no one prisoner take away more than one pint of water at a time, but they had two or three copper ladles chained to the cask from which we were allowed to drink as much as we wanted. The old marines, being long on board and stationary, the faces of the prisoners had become familiar to them [which] put it in their power to detect fraud, which was often practiced by the prisoners to procure water to carry below for cooking purposes [which was] not allowed of by the ship's regulations, and over the water our soldiers had no control. They worked while on guard with muskets for other purposes.

But to return to the subject of water, it may be necessary to observe that our daily consumption of this article was at least seven hundred gallons per day on board the *Jersey*. I know not whence it was brought but probably from Brooklyn, and it was the constant employment of a large gondola or large undecked shallop to bring it alongside, and the working party was always partly employed in taking it on board. What was not taken on board and upon deck for immediate use was conducted into the lower hold of the hulk through a leather hose made for that purpose, the outside or receiving part being near the ship's bend, from whence it was now conducted into large butts fixed to receive it, where it remained as a reservoir to which we had recourse when we had no other.

The water at best was very brackish, but that from the ship's hold was nauseous. It could not be otherwise, [for] the butts which contained it had never been cleansed since they were first placed there for this purpose. The sediment must in the course of so long a time have become very great, and every time that water was [poured] into the butts, it disturbed this sediment [which] became incorporated with the water, which rendered it of the most disgusting and poisonous nature, and I have no doubt upon my own mind [that it] has been the cause of the death of hundreds of the prisoners. To allay the tormenting thirst, they were reduced to the necessity of having recourse to this liquid poison for their immediate preservation and abide by the event. When better water was brought on board, no one who had not been there can have any conception of the struggle to procure a draught of pure water.[39]

> *While yet they deign'd that healthy juice to lade*
> *The putrid water felt its powerful aid;*
> *But when refus'd–to aggravate our pains–*
> *Then fever rag'd and revel'd through our veins.*
> [Freneau]

The Bumboat

There was but one indulgence allowed us by our keepers, if it may be so called. That was a permission for a boat to come alongside of the *Jersey* with some necessaries to supply the prisoners, at least such as had the means to purchase. This boat

39. Apparently the quality of water varied considerably, since the narratives differ somewhat from one another on this matter. It may be, as Dring suggests, that the nearby sources of good fresh water tended to dry up in the summer, necessitating the hauling of water from a greater distance, or in a pinch using the stale and dirty water stored in the ship's hold. See Dawson's note in Dring-Greene, *Recollections*, 71–72. Concerning the quantity of the water, a daily consumption of seven hundred gallons for about one thousand prisoners would allow each prisoner something over two-thirds of a gallon, perhaps just enough for drinking and cooking, but certainly not sufficient for washing of body or clothes. Apparently water was never a problem in the other New York or English prisons. See the sources listed in notes 16 and 19 to the editor's introduction.

was called the bumboat, and the trade [was] conducted by a very corpulent old woman whom the prisoners called Dame Grant, and it was told us that she was aunt to the commissary of prisoners (David Sproat).[40] Be this as it may, it was an accommodation to us, and, I presume, a lucrative trade to Dame Grant. She came from New York every other day with her well selected articles of trade such as sugar, tea, soft bread, fruit, etc., all of which was ready in parcels done up in paper from one pound to one ounce, the price already affixed on them, from which there was no deviation.

The old lady sat in the stern sheets of the boat (which her bulk completely filled). She had with her two boys to row the boat and hand us the article we wanted, first receiving the money for it. We were sometimes allowed to descend to the bottom of the accommodation ladder to the boat for this purpose, that is if our guard was not a refugee. The box of goods was placed before Dame Grant, and she served us very expeditiously.

While making our purchase, it was lamentable to see hundreds of poor, starving wretches looking over the side into the boat, viewing with hankering the contents which they had it not in their power to purchase, no, not even a piece of good bread or anything else that they then saw and which they undoubtedly had a short time before their captivity had in abundance. There was none among us who had the means of supplying their wants even if we had the disposition to do it. I never seemed to enjoy what I had procured for my own comfort from this boat on this very account, seeing so many needy [men] gazing at the purchase made, who seemed almost dying for the want of it. It was distressing to see them and know their sufferings. Their condition has already been described, and I

40. Dame Grant is not mentioned in any other narrative. Her being related to David Sproat remains conjecture.

must leave them in wretchedness, though the scene can never be lost sight of by the writer.

But to return to the accommodation of this boat and the old lady who commanded her, we looked out with anxiety [for] the approach of Dame Grant, expecting such things as we had given her [a] memorandum to procure for us, such as pipes, tobacco, snuff, thread, needles, paper, hair combs, and many other things of which we stood in need, all of which she assured us we had at cost. But alas, how shortly were our lives and our enjoyments thus cut off at once [from] our usual supplies by the death of Dame Grant, who took the contagion from us and died, and although not in the flower of [her] youth, it was in the time of usefulness to us prisoners, and we regretted her loss, which was never after supplied.[41]

The Sutler [and other Subjects]

Being deprived of the benefit of purchasing from the bumboat as just stated, we had recourse to the sutler, so called. This was one of the mates of the *Jersey*, who sold to the prisoners many things of which they were in want, particularly ardent spirits, which article was not allowed to be brought alongside by any conveyance whatever but could be procured from him at two dollars per gallon. His storeroom was abaft the bulkhead of the quarterdeck, through which was a scuttle cut. We handed him the money first, and he gave what he pleased. There was no

41. The bumboat system did not begin or end with Dame Grant. It was a regular part of life on the *Jersey,* though of course only for those who could pay. See, for instance, Alexander Coffin Jr. to Dr. Samuel L. Mitchell, September 4, 1807, printed in Dawson's appendix, Dring-Greene, *Recollections,* 184; *Memoirs of Andrew Sherburne,* 113. The British claimed that it was possible for prisoners to go ashore daily to purchase goods (*Report on Treatment of Naval Prisoners* by Captain G. Dawson and other British naval officers, February 2, 1781, printed in Banks, *David Sproat,* 53). Jeremiah Johnson, who lived as a boy at the time on the shore of the Wallabout, states that prisoners helping

bargain to make on our part, [but] to such as had money, even this mode of purchasing was considered an accommodation.[42]

The greatest difficulty that we labored under was to procure wood to cook with, and this could not be purchased from him or anyone else. It is true that the cook's mates stole some and sold it to us at the hazard of being punished, but the demand was so great that their embezzlements could no way supply our necessity. Everyone who could procure wood by any means sought after it to avoid eating what was cooked in the ship's copper (as before stated in the former part of this narrative).

I omitted to mention in its proper place my good luck in picking up, on my excursion on shore upon the occasion of a funeral, a hogshead stave in the surface of the water which I was permitted to take up and carry on board (our guard being Hessians). This was truly a treasure to me and to the mess to

haul water from a nearby spring came to his father's house and to Mr. Remsen's to procure food. Jeremiah's father also reportedly delivered letters for them, and occasionally gave them money (*Recollections of Brooklyn and New York*, printed in Dawson's appendix, 191). None of these activities is mentioned by Dring, and it seems probable that few benefited from them. A similar system prevailed at the prisons in England, where a market of sorts operated at the gates of the prison. The difference was in the amount of money spent, and the number and quality of goods available. In England the prisoners were receiving regular weekly donations much of the time, as well as money for handicraft goods they sold, and whatever other donations they could secure from sympathetic British visitors. No such opportunities existed in the prison ships. Unlike the situation in New York, local merchants in Plymouth and Portsmouth, England, who had no reason to fear approaching the prisons, who saw a good source of regular profit, and who might have been sympathetic toward the Americans, gladly sold to the prisoners there.

42. The sutler, unlike the bumboat, is not mentioned in other narratives. His apparently clandestine liquor business must have depended for its existence upon his superiors' shutting their eyes (for a price probably) to this violation of regulations, and thus may have been a sporadic service.

which I belonged and served us for a long time in the economical way that it was used, but while I am upon the subject of wood, it may not be here improper to say that I was truly fortunate in this respect, as I had an abundant supply while I was on board for myself and a little to spare sometimes to a distressed neighbor.

My good luck proceeded from the following circumstance. I had one day the command of the working party. On this day we took in a sloop-load of wood (for the ship's men). The wood was passed below under a guard to prevent embezzlement. I, however, by the help of my associates, found means to get a cleft of wood as big as a man's thigh and got it safely conveyed into the gun room and properly secreted. Our mess was now amply supplied, and I considered myself the principal proprietor of this treasure, and our mess was considered the most wealthy of any in this republic of misery. We had now the satisfaction to supply our next neighbor occasionally with a few splinters, they getting it of themselves with a jack knife which was the only mode that we had to reduce it into pieces of about four inches long. This operation took up much of our time and was the work by turns of the whole mess, and we were happy in the employment.[43]

After we had by dint of industry gotten the wood into splinters, it was put into the chest for [the] next occasion. In the meanwhile, the main stack was duly guarded by night and by day. It was of too much value to ever be out of sight. We always had it in our enclosure by night, and every precaution [was] used for its safety. So much did we prize it that we even made mathematical calculations [of] how long it would last us at the

43. It is worth noticing the temporary change in Dring's tone. "Beating the system" was obviously a source of gratification, which even led him to use the word "happy." Although his usually somber tone reflects a sense of helplessness, here is one of a few examples of positive self-help, which served to buoy the spirits.

rate we used it per day. It may be thought by some that I have dwelt too long upon this trifling subject, but my motive was only to show what a value may be put upon a trifling thing, particularly situated as we were, and [its] importance to us at the time and place of abode. The flint is sometimes of more value to the possessor than a diamond would be of the same magnitude.

> But such a train of endless woes abound,
> So many mischiefs in these hulks are found,
> That on them all a poem to prolong
> Would swell too high the horrors of my song–
> [Freneau]

Our confined and limited space within the wooden walls of this ponderous, odious hulk would admit of no recreation. How different was the fate of those American prisoners who were sent to England at that time and put into Forton and Mill Prisons so called, the place of their confinement. It was absolutely a paradise compared to that of the old *Jersey*. They were confined, it is true, but they had a spacious yard to walk in and a place for manly recreation by day and a light afforded them by night. They were all in good health. They had plenty of wholesome water, not only to drink but for cooking and other purposes, and their provisions, what they had, were fresh and good. They could procure vegetables and everything they wanted for their comfort. They received many donations from the well disposed, and [there was] an agent to supply them with decent clothing, and their complaints could be attended to, and more than all, they had no putrid fevers prevailing among them.[44]

44. Although Dring's description of the English prisons as comparative paradises is overdrawn, he does have a correct sense of the fact that life in these prisons was much easier than life on the *Jersey*. See the sources listed in note 19 to the editor's introduction; see also comparative comments in notes 20, 26–27, 31, 33, 39, 41, 45, 47, 49, 50, 53, 54, and 56.

I mention those circumstances to show the difference. Only view our deplorable condition on board the *Jersey* already described, and upon our own waters. But oh, my country, why did you neglect us in this our time of distress, why not contribute to afford the dying victims only a little food and raiment? Our foes would have permitted the donation to be duly appropriated. With what joy and rapture it [would] have been accepted by us poor, half-starved wretches then suffering in one common cause, and we very justly accused our country of a total neglect toward us in our then deplorable condition and cast many reflections on those whose business it was to attend to our repeated supplications.[45] But further observations upon their ingratitude would carry my remarks beyond my present intentions.

I have, however, the satisfaction to find that after a lapse of twenty-five years, their precious bones, these relics of departed

45. There is indeed a contrast between the American population, which virtually ignored the prisoners at the Wallabout, and the sympathetic elements of the British population, who, for instance, in a few weeks in December 1777 and January 1778, raised over £3,000 as a donation to the American prisoners, and later, when the fund ran dry, repeated the campaign. In the English prisons there were also monthly clothing inspections, and prisoners actually reported occasionally turning down unneeded clothing offered to them. At holiday times special donations of food were made. The prisoners grew so much to expect these "extras" that they complained bitterly when they were not forthcoming. Here is a good measure of the difference between *Jersey* and English prison life. See the sources listed in note 19 to the editor's introduction. American "negligence" can be explained in several ways. The loyalists in New York were probably more hostile to American prisoners than the British home population. Also, the prison ships had such a bad reputation of filth and disease that most people probably stayed as far away as possible. Access by more sympathetic Americans was made extremely difficult by the British, despite Dring's wishful thinking to the contrary. Finally, the struggling central government of the United States, which did attempt to send food and clothing to official military prisoners, seems to have found it impossible to supply basic necessities to the thousands of privateer prisoners.

men who died in the cause of their country, who withstood every privation that is possible for men to endure, as the pen [has] described, yet it shook not their fortitude nor induced them to forsake their country's cause, those dry bones [which had] withstood the bleaching of the stormy winters and summer's scorching sun, have, however, since received the rights of sepulture which had been denied to their remains for so long a time, and "the time has come when they shall rest in the tomb of their fathers . . . and here shall the tear of sensibility flow for their sufferings" [De Witt, 83].[46]

[Bylaws]

But to return to my narrative, our ancestors in suffering who first entered these desolate mansions (and whose precious bones are probably among those just described) had very wisely adopted a code of bylaws for the regulation and government among the prisoners, which had been complied with ever since they were enacted, that is, as far as circumstances would admit of. I regret that I cannot here give them verbatim, but they in part have slipped my recollection. But they principally were calculated to preserve our health and morality by cleanliness. A noncompliance to those regulations [resulted in] a penalty or a punishment, and it is astonishing to observe how long this order had prevailed among us, considering how numerous we were, and a class of people supposedly not easily controlled or disposed to good order, and notwithstanding [the fact that] our numbers consisted of many foreigners over whom we had no control, yet they (much to their credit) followed our good example and seemed disposed to a compliance as far as their condition would admit of.

46. See page 124 and note 4. The passage above also contains free paraphrasing of material from the Tammany Society Wallabout Committee's *Report* of February 1, 1808, printed in Vandervoort, *Account*, 14.

Our bylaws forbade us smoking below by day or night. This was absolutely necessary on account of the sick. Cleanliness in our persons was strongly recommended and complied with as far as our condition or means would admit of. Profane language was forbidden, and sobriety was strongly recommended. Theft was punishable, and a recommendation [was made] to all on board to refrain from recreation on the Sabbath and to appear on that day shaved. The officers [were] to set the example and the sailors to follow it as far as they had it in their power, but it was to be lamented that they had not the means to appear well clothed, but there was no want on their part of due subordination.[47]

Our bylaws were sometimes read to the prisoners, particularly when anyone was to be punished for any violation of them, which was sometimes put in execution, the oldest officer among the prisoners presiding as judge. Theft or fraud upon a prisoner's allowance, if detected, was always punished by cobbing [a form of beating with a corncob or lump of coal (called a cob)?] upon the forecastle and universally approved of.

[Our Orator and his Discourse]

We never had any preaching, praying, or psalm singing while I was on board the *Jersey*, nor were we ever favored with a visit from any of the clergy. We were neglected in every respect. But we had a sailor on board who was a singular character and an extraordinary orator. I knew not from whence he came [*sic*; see page 72], but he certainly, from his eloquence and address, had the appearance of having the benefit of a very good education.

---

47. This is an interesting display of self-government, and not a unique example. Andrew Sherburne describes the establishment of a constitution and laws among the prisoners at Old Mill Prison at Plymouth, England, early in 1782 (*Memoirs of Andrew Sherburne*, 83). Dring's comment about "due subordination" reflects his day's gentlemanly and paternalistic political philosophy.

He told us that he had been a very bad youth, that he had quit his family, contrary to their advice, and that their predictions had been verified, that is, that the old *Jersey* would bring him up, and the bank [would] be his place of interment. The first, he observed, had come to pass, and he was prepared for the event of the other. Death had with him lost its terrors, and to it he had become familiarized.

On several occasions he harangued the prisoners upon a Sunday morning. His discourse made a suitable impression upon my mind and upon my memory. He would mount upon a small eminence upon the spar deck and with a laudable voice would summon all to assemble and to attend to the word of truth, which was always complied with on the part of the prisoners, and silence and due attention to his discourse was duly observed. He then told us that our present assemblage was not by way of derision or mockery [of it] being Sunday, but that the good order prevailing among us had induced us to refrain from all recreation upon this sacred day [and] that his object was not to preach to us nor say anything upon the subject of scripture. He only proposed to read to us the bylaws, which he then held in his hand and the framers of which were probably deposited under yonder bank (pointing to the shore). [He said that] they were founded in wisdom and well calculated to maintain order and decorum among us, [that] they had heretofore been strictly complied with in every respect, and [that] his present motive in having them assemble was to repeat the necessity of a due adherence to them, which he would read, and to make some observations upon their utility so far as respected us in our present condition, and that each paragraph might be called his text.

Our orator expounded upon each and every article of our bylaws. He dwelt copiously upon all parts and pointed out clearly the absolute necessity of our strict adherence to them and the bad consequences which would certainly result from a neglect of them. Attention to order, cleanliness, and morality was duly recommended. The great enormity of intemperance and theft was pointed out to us in all its heinousness as a disgrace to all people and particularly to us on the brink of the grave. Profane language, he said, could be well dispensed with at present, as we were doing penance in purgatory.

He then observed that our present punishment was (in his opinion) the result of our former transgressions and that the Almighty had been pleased in his wisdom to adopt this mode of punishment for us and that his infernal majesty, the devil, had been permitted to send his agents out in every direction to collect us together and that by their vigilance all that he saw then before him, and many more, had been the result of those instructions, and we were the victims. He recommended to us to bear up under our present confinement and all the aggravating tortures of body and mind, as it was only atonement for our transgressions, and assured us that once having passed through this furnace, all our sins were forgiven us and that our residence on board the old *Jersey* would compensate fully for all, be their magnitude what they would, and that we should bear in mind as consolation that no punishment hereafter was to be inflicted upon us for the past, but [that] still we might by our own indiscretion accumulate another load and merit it, but upon which subject he should then be silent.

He then made some very just and suitable observations upon our fortitude in bearing up under all our sufferings and not forsaking the banner of our country and by our sufferings being induced to enter the service of our enemy, notwithstanding the inducement. While he was thus speaking, the sentinels upon the gangway would shorten their pace and listen attentively to his discourse. We were fearful that he would by his remarks bring upon himself their resentment and cautioned him on that subject. But he observed that they could do nothing more except put him to the torture. He further said that among the devil's principal agents was David Sproat, commissary of prisoners, and that he was called "hell's tormentor." He finally concluded by exhorting the virtues of the fallen victims who had already paid the debt of nature and joined those martyred saints in the celestial abodes.

Our orator then told us that the time would come when their precious bones would all be collected and have the rites of sepulture and that a monument would be erected to their memories whose base should be founded in hell among our foes and whose summit should reach the heavens among our martyred saints in commemoration of the fallen heroes who fell victims to British barbarity on board their prison ships in New York in vindication of their rights and the rights of man, and it is with pleasure that I can say that his predictions have been fully verified. A monument has been erected suitable to the occasion near the spot where their bones were collected at the Wallabout, and [they were] humanely deposited with that reverence and solemnity which was due on this very interesting occasion, which will be described hereafter.[48]

> *The days to come shall to your memory raise*
> *Piles on those shores to spread through earth your praise.*

Our orator's name was Cooper and was a Virginian and only a common sailor (to appearance), but he was certainly a young man of very great abilities, and his discourse was well adapted to our situation. I remember we attempted to call him Elder or Parson Cooper, but he told us we must not accost him by that salutation, and if we were disposed to give him a distinguished title from that of sailor, he would consent to be called Doctor,

---

48. See page 124. Actually, on the occasion in 1808 to which he is referring, no monument was erected. Nor was a monument constructed until a century later, by which time the bones (in 1873) had been taken from the 1808 wooden sepulcher, and reinterred in a brick vault in Fort Greene Park in Brooklyn.

by which he was ever after saluted. He made many remarks upon the neglect of our well disposed and pious clergy who had so much concern for our precious souls. "Not one," says he, "has ever entered those bodes of wretchedness to afford one cheering ray of hope or to administer the Gospel to us." He presumed there was no obstacle in the way if they were disposed to visit us, no, not even David Sproat would oppose it, as bad as he was. "But no, fellow sufferers," says he, "that is not the difficulty. The want of a reward for the service of their pious services is the obstacle in part." They foresaw that their fare would be hard (if any) and [that] the hazard [was great] of taking the fever which was well known to all the country to prevail among us, and [that] the vermin would stick to them (for they always preferred fresh meat). [This] was sufficient reason why they, those soul saving and disinterested men, never on one solitary instance made us a visit while I was there.[49]

But I shall here drop this subject and only say a few words more as respects our orator, for whom I had a high regard at the time and have since often thought of, and if I knew he was living, I would make my acknowledgement to him for his services and sincerely hope he may be placed in a more desirable situation than we were when together on board the old *Jersey*.

He remained three months among us. A stranger one day came on board, accompanied by the commissary of prisoners, and Cooper was inquired for and summoned. When he appeared, a letter was put into his hand, and having perused it, he left the ship immediately without even going below after his things, and the boat put off toward New York. There were various conjectures upon the manner of his sudden departure. Some said that poor Cooper had drawn upon himself the

49. No mention whatever is made in any of the narratives of American prisoners at New York or in England of any religious activities.

vengeance of old Sproat and that he had then taken him onshore to punish him. But I believe that, being of some respectable and influential family, his friends had procured his release. This was often done through the influence of the royalists or refugees at New York, for they might have been formerly friends and neighbors to those who made the application to them in behalf of their son or friend then in captivity, and although they might differ in their present political opinions and [had] taken each a different part in the contest, yet [they] were disposed to render each other their services in the mutual way above mentioned.

He waved his hand as he left the ship and bade us to be of good cheer. We could only reply by the same salutation. Thus we lost our orator, from whom I have never since heard. It was somewhat extraordinary that among such a multitude of men, there was no one that ever attempted to exhort except the one just mentioned. Each was employed in his own preservation.

We had but few amusements except gambling. Every chest or box had a chequerboard cut or painted upon it, and [there were] plenty of dirty cards among us. To those amusements, if they may be so called, the prisoners devoted much of their time. We had many very ingenious people among us, and many extraordinary pieces of workmanship were performed by them, though it was with great difficulty that they could there procure the materials to work with, our principal commodity being dried bones and our tools only a knife and a piece of glass or some trifling thing to polish with, and this was wholly by way of amusement.[50] Thus day after day we passed

50. In contrast to the handiwork done on the *Jersey*, the captives in English prisons were given materials to make goods such as boxes, ladles, spoons, and chairs, which they sold to sympathetic British visitors. Charles Herbert's diary, *Relic of the Revolution,* describes particularly well the boxes he made, how much money he received for them, and how charitable his buyers were for purchasing such useless items.

our lingering time by light and our anxious nights in utter darkness, groping our way as our occasions might require among the carcasses which bestrewed the deck, their only place of repose.

4th of July [and its Aftermath]

> But what on captives British rage can do,
> Another Canto, friend, shall let you know.
> [Freneau]

Previous to our anniversary of independence (4th of July), the prisoners had made such preparation as their needy circumstances would then admit of to celebrate the day. In innocent past time, as they had procured something to make themselves merry upon the occasion, they never dreamt that our foes would take an umbrage at our proceedings, as they had no intentions of insulting them. As prisoners, we thought that we had a right to sing or be merry upon this day at least. As soon as we were permitted to come upon deck, a number of little national flags were displayed along upon the booms, that is, thirteen, and in a short time we were directed by the guards to take them away, which, however, was not complied with by the prisoners, and they triumphantly demolished them and trod them under foot. This heroic deed was witnessed on the part of the prisoners with that contempt the transaction so justly merited, but nothing was uttered by us to give offense, that is, not intentionally. A number of patriotic songs were sung in the course of the time we were on deck and choruses were repeated.

Unfortunately for us, we had at this time a guard of detestable Scotchmen who, next to the refugees, were our worst enemies. They were evidently displeased at the transaction as will hereafter appear.

Remembrance shudders at this scene of fears–
Still in my view some English brute appears,
Some base-born Hessian slave walks threat'ning by,
Some servile Scot with murder in his eye
Still haunts my sight, as vainly they bemoan
Rebellions manag'd so unlike their own.
[Freneau]

Their moroseness was a harbinger to what was to follow. We were not permitted to pass the common gangway as usual, and an attempt to do it [meant] a prick of the bayonet. Thus ill commoded, the prisoners had no redress. They still continued their mirth and some cheering. The guards were now turned out, and their murdering countenances bespoke their cruel intentions, for we were ordered to descend to the between decks immediately and at the point of the bayonet at 4 o'clock in hate and confusion.

"Down, rebels, down!" the angry Scotchmen cry,
"Damn'd dogs, descend or by our broad swords die!"
[Freneau]

Having driven us all below at this unusual and unprecedented hour and [with] the gratings laid upon us, we concluded that all had been done to satiate their bloodthirsty views and that they had reached the grand climax of their barbarity. But they seemed to exult in the luxury of human woes. Oh, "why fell not the red bolt of Heaven on the heads of those monsters in the shape of men? Why did the vengeance of God sleep for a moment upon their bloody crimes? [But] dark and mysterious are the ways of Providence, and cannot be questioned!" [Fay, 56–57].

Such murdering deeds your murdering host declaim [?];
We grieve to think, their form and ours, the same.

But they had other punishment in view and only awaited the signal to put their vengeance in execution. The prisoners below continued to be merry and perhaps noisy, though they forbore to give any aggravating expressions (that I heard or knew of) except [if] patriotic songs could be so construed. We were now enveloped in darkness when we were ordered to desist from any noise, which, however, was not duly complied with on the part of the prisoners. About 9 o'clock the gratings were unlaid, and the guards descended with drawn cutlasses and lanterns to benefit their cloudy intentions. Those poor, helpless men retreated upon their approach, that is, as far as their limited and crowded situation would admit of. They pursued the wretched fugitives as far as their cowardice dared to do, cutting all whom they could reach, and again ascended the deck after their glorious exploit, exulting in their bloody transaction by which it seems their revenge was in some measure accomplished. Many were wounded among us, but to what number or extent could not be ascertained in the utter darkness which then surrounded us. But the cries and groans throughout this tragical night were dreadful indeed.

> *The dead were past their pain, the living groan,*
> *Nor dare to hope another morn their own.*
> [Freneau]

For my own part, I was far removed from this scene of human woe and terror, [in the gun room,] but the general lamentation which echoed throughout the ship could not but enter my ear, and execrations throughout this dismal night upon the heads of our vindictive foe were heard from every direction. They even challenged or invited their assailants to make another murderous attempt among them, which they, however, had the precaution not to do or the cowardice not to venture [below] even armed as they were.

It was truly a night of anxiety and apprehensions, and sleep to me was that night a stranger. The heat was excessive, and I passed the dismal hours at the grating as I had frequently done before to inhale the sweet air. My station was on the larboard side facing toward the East. From this situation I could observe the stars rise and progress in their height until their altitude became too great to be further seen and another succeeded in a more horizontal position to attract our attention. Thus we pass our nights and beguile our time until the returning hours of day unbar the gate of light and let forth the morn.

> *Dull flew the hours, till, from the East display'd,*
> *Sweet morn dispelled the horrors of the shade.*
> [Freneau]

It had been customary for the prisoners to take down with them a pint of water previous to their being turned below at night to quench their thirst or use as occasion might require, but on this fatal day we had been driven down precipitantly at 4 o'clock, that is, three hours before the setting sun in a very hot day without a drop of water. The thirst upon this occasion was extreme throughout the night. The cries for a drop of water resounded from every part of the between decks but cannot be described by me.

> *"Here, generous Britain, generous, as you say,*
> *"To my parch'd tongue one cooling drop convey,*
> *"Hell has no mischief like a thirsty throat,*
> *"Nor one tormentor like your David Sproat."*
> [Freneau]

I have before mentioned that the commissary of prisoners was David Sproat, an American refugee (of detested memory). It was by his instigation or order that we were thus inhumanly treated upon this and other occasions, and to him may be just-ly attributed all our sufferings on this fatal night. (But it was said that this wretch, after the peace, was hanged in London, not for his good deeds, but the gallows claimed her own.)[51]

The English dwelt much upon the treatment that their subjects experienced by Tippoo Sahib at Calcutta when seventy of them were placed in a small space and suffocation was the consequence to part of them,[52] but they had no compassion upon us poor, dying, supplicating prisoners, a thousand in number, imploring their humanity, to which they paid no regard. Thus with those tormenting cravings for water and air and [with] the "darkness [rolling] about the head of the captive–'silent he listens to the sounding' [noise]–and sighs as he thinks on the high-bosomed partner of his heart. He rises in the fury of his madness, and hopes for means to escape. Alas! there is no [escape]." There is no hope to cheer his bewildered mind. "The unfeeling sentinel, faithful to his trust, paces the deck with an ever watchful eye–the prisoner groans out his life unpitied, unattended!–and the watchman halloos to the passing hour of night, that 'all is well'! . . . Think, fellow-citizens, what would be your sensations were you thus [situated and suffering] in your country's cause? And . . . ye [fair] daughters of America . . . how could you bear to reflect on the [sufferings] of a [father, a brother, or a] lover thus [situated]?" Yet ye have, many of you whose grandsires were among the number of the sufferers, a circumstance to which perhaps you may be totally unacquainted at this time. But it comes within my rec-

51. Dring apparently has confused the fate of David Sproat, who died of natural causes in Scotland in 1799 (see note 17), with the supposed fate of Captain William Cunningham, Provost Marshall of the provost prison at New York, who is said to have been hanged in England in 1791 for embezzlement (see note 32).

52. It is not clear whether Dring is referring here to the famous Black Hole of Calcutta atrocity, which took place in 1756, or to a lesser known but similar atrocity perpetrated by Tipoo Sahib, who with French help unsuccessfully fought the Second Mysore War against the British between 1781 and 1784.

ollection, and if their names are not particularly mentioned, their virtues shall be recorded, for "they preferred a terrible death to a dereliction of principle" [Fay, 58-59].

> *Hail, dark abode! what can with thee compare–*
> *Heat, sickness, famine, death, and stagnant air–*
> [Freneau]

The morning at length returned, for which we had waited with the greatest anxiety and flattered ourselves that we should be permitted to ascend the deck at our usual hour and allay our thirst, but the gratings not being unlaid at the usual time for the working party to ascend to their duty for which purpose they were then in waiting at the hatchway, this circumstance filled our minds with sorrowful forebodings, and hour after hour passed heavily on, and our sufferings increasing with the delay, we now began to think that they had concluded to make one finishing stroke with us and at once terminate our wretched existence and rid themselves of the trouble of us altogether.

However, at about 10 o'clock on the 5th of July we had the pleasure to find the gratings were unbarred, and we were permitted to ascend the deck once more, everyone making toward the water cask. But there was not sufficient [water] at hand to allay our thirst. The crowd was so great to obtain a drop of water that the guard was again turned out to disperse us. A few hours [wait], however, produced a supply, but it was one continual application at the cask throughout the day.

We had no fire in the caboose [galley] this day, [so] of course we had nothing to eat except what we ate raw. Our provision or allowance was served out to us but not at the usual hour. Everything was deranged by the event of last night's proceedings. Indeed, it was several days before harmony was restored, which was finally produced by the change of the guard [which] to our joy was composed of Hessians. They appeared to have a little compassion for us and would sometimes say "poor rebels." Those Scotch scoundrels seemed to exult in our misery, and to humanity they were utter strangers.

We had every reason to suppose that the morning's sight would produce an additional number of dead. When the between decks were cleared out as usual, there were eight or ten found dead and brought up and laid upon the gratings. It did not appear that any was killed by the proceedings of the evening before, but a number were wounded upon that fatal event whose wounds could not be attended to during the night in utter darkness, and even the next day they had no further assistance than what could be rendered by their fellow prisoners who had nothing to administer for their comfort, nor bandages to dress their wounds. I, however, knew none among the dead or wounded, but the dead were as customary conveyed onshore by the boat from the *Hunter* and deposited under the bank. This uncommon number of the dead was doubtless owing in a great measure to the scene of the last night and produced by that event. Our usual number used to be about four or five to die in the space of twenty-four hours upon an average on board the *Jersey*. In this instance it was double and exceeded anyone case while I was among them.[53]

> *Where death in tenfold vengeance holds his reign,*
> *And injur'd ghosts, yet unaveng'd, complain;*
> *This be my task–ungenerous Britons, you*
> *Conspire to murder whom you can't subdue.–*
> [Freneau]

53. Dring's estimate of four or five as a normal average of deaths per day is, if anything, low in comparison to other narratives, some of whose estimates run higher than ten per day (see, for instance, Caritat, *Silas Talbot*, 109). By way of contrast, during Charles Herbert's entire stay of over two years at the Old Mill Prison in Plymouth, England, only twenty-one prisoners died, though of course those twenty-one were as much lamented as cruel and unnecessary deaths as those on the *Jersey* (see *Relic of the Revolution*). Also see note 6.

In committing what I have related through this work to paper, there has undoubtedly been a want of order, but being the spontaneous effusion of the moment and the recollection of such events as took place from time to time, the occurrences crowd rapidly upon my memory, although a lapse of more than forty years has since passed away, but such was the impression made at the time, and a continual recollection of the events has had a tendency to keep them in mind. Often have I since, while pacing the deck of a good ship under my command, viewing the rising stars and recollecting my viewing the same through the iron gratings of the old *Jersey* when their progress served to beguile the dreary night and were seen from a deplorable situation when compared to my present condition where I have my liberty, my health, and every worldly comfort. I cannot but reflect upon the contrast and bless the Being from which they have been derived. I have never regretted my captivity nor my sufferings. It has had a tendency to make me enjoy [a] life which otherwise I perhaps should not have known, and recording the scene affords me a gratification in doing it.

Effect of Smoking

I have before mentioned that among our bylaws was one which forbade smoking below deck by day or by night, but being much in the habit of smoking myself, I must confess that it would have been then considered a great luxury to me to have had this indulgence, in a particular manner by night while placed at the gratings for the smell of the sweet air. But it was not admissible, and I was reconciled to the prohibition, and we waited with great impatience for the pleasing moment when we should be permitted to ascend the deck and to again enjoy the pleasure of smoking. It had now become a universal practice among the prisoners, that is, such of us as could procure the means, and as soon as fire could be procured, we went at our favorite amusement.

We were not allowed to have any fire works among us, and the fire was first procured from the cook (to the ship's officers) through a small window or scuttle in the bulkhead near his caboose. Having once procured fire, we took it from each other, as we dared not make individual applications to procure it, as this surly scoundrel would not afford it. One morning I applied my face to this hole and asked for fire. The miscreant, without making any reply, threw a shovel of cinders in my face. It almost blinded me and gave me great pain, and it was several days before I could regain my sight.

The reader may judge what were my sensations upon this occasion. Redress was out of the question, as we were never allowed to have any mode of seeking it. I only mention this circumstance to show to what a state of degradation we were reduced [by them] from their commissary down to their cooks and the cook's scullion. Perhaps this transaction would not have been justified by the commander, but we had no means whereby we could have redress for any cruelties inflicted upon us. As their servants, they ought in justice to have listened to our complaints and [to have] made it known that our grievances should be attended to, the aggressor to meet his deserts. This would at once have put a stop to many vexations and acts of cruelty which we experienced from those miscreants.[54]

54. Dring is right that no formal grievance procedure existed for the *Jersey* prisoners to use. Prisoners did, however, address petitions and letters for relief to the world at large through the newspapers (see note 27). This publicity, along with official complaints from American military leaders, was enough to keep British officials busy defending their policies in reply. Probably the complaints kept conditions from worsening under British leaders who otherwise might have been glad to ignore the prison ship situation. See, for instance, Abraham Skinner to David Sproat, June 24, 1782, and Sproat's reply, June 30, 1782, both printed in Dawson's appendix, Dring-Greene, *Recollections*, 147–53. See also Dawson's appendix, 129–34, 138–45, 153–57; Onderdonk, *Revolutionary Incidents,* 233–44; Banks, *David Sproat,* 34–67, 72–101; Bushnell's notes in *Adventures of Christopher Hawkins,* 260–62;

But to return to our smoking enjoyment, when we got into full operation, a cloud of smoke arose and seemed to clarify the pestilential air with which we were surrounded, and it was to this habit of smoking that I attribute in great measure the preservation of my health while on board the old *Jersey*. The greatest and only difficulty was to procure the tobacco, and to many who had not the means, it must have been an aggravation to see others puffing away their sorrows and apparently leaving their grief behind, but for my own part, I experienced no want on this account and enjoyed the luxury.

An Attempt at Escape [and the Consequences]

It would be almost needless to recount the many vexations and cruelties we daily experienced from those petty tyrants who were placed over us, and to tantalize our misery, a prick from the bayonet or a push from the gangway had become familiar to us, and we were obliged to abide the consequence.

> *No favours could these sons of death bestow,*
> *'Twas endless cursing, and continual woe:*
> *Immoral hatred doth their breasts engage,*
> *And this lost empire swells their souls with rage.*
> [Freneau]

But to relate the cruelties which we were subjected to by ill treatment (exclusive of starvation) would swell this narrative much beyond my first intention. I, however, cannot refrain

Dandridge, *American Prisoners*, 399–431. In the English prisons, by way of contrast, the prison officials at Old Mill Prison at least once accepted a petition from the prisoners and made some improvements based upon prisoner demands. See "Diary of William Widger," *Essex Institute Historical Collections* 74:142. Furthermore, prisoner petitions found their way into the debates in Parliament on the subject of American prisoner treatment. See, for instance, the British *Annual Register*, 1781, 152, quoted in Jeremiah Johnson's *Recollections of Brooklyn and New York*, printed in Dawson's appendix, 192.

from relating one circumstance which took place to which I was a witness while I was there and then drop the subject as respects our deplorable condition and leave it to the reader to form some idea of the magnitude of our complaints and wretchedness.

The prisoners in the gun room had it in contemplation to make their escape by cutting through the stern, or rather the counter of the ship, which they put in execution by cutting through oak planks of hard wood four inches thick without a tool to accomplish it but one gimlet and their jack knives.[55] This was certainly a mad undertaking on their part, but such was their desire to once more obtain their liberty than nothing was thought impracticable by them, and they commenced their work. Having first placed a blanket suspended betwixt the workman and those without by way of their concealment, the business was commenced and constantly pursued by us all in rotation, partly by way of assistance and partly for our amusement.

For my own part, I never had any intentions of then joining the project, and however great my desires were to obtain my liberty, I knew this mode was impossible to effect it. I, however, assisted in the task and sincerely wished the projectors might fully realize their wish for liberation by making their escape. We finally, by diligence and perseverance, by cutting from seam to seam through those hard planks, got through to a very fine shell so that the piece could be gotten through in a few minutes whenever a suitable time offered [itself] to put their plan in execution. Among the intended adventurers was a young man, mate of a ship from Philadelphia (I think his

---

55. A sailing ship's counter is the portion of the hull from the waterline upward to the extreme outward swell, or overhang of the stern. A gimlet is a small tool with a screw point, grooved shank, and cross handle, for boring holes.

name was Lawrence), with whom I had formed a particular acquaintance, [he] being my next neighbor or adjoining companion by messing.

It may not here be unnecessary to repeat that our little enclosures made by our chests and boxes etc. where we assembled to eat and sleep formed a little kind of republic, and the next mess was of course our nearest neighbor, and we borrowed [from] and lent [to] each other like good women in a sociable neighborhood and were always ready to bestow mutual services toward each other as far as our abilities would admit of. Our mutual sufferings seemed to operate like a cement among us. For the whole time that I was among them, I never knew any contention whatever.

It was in this laudable intention that we all (in the gun room) assisted in cutting out, although we principally did disapprove of it, well knowing that in all probability escape could not be then effected, and the obstacles to the undertaking were duly set forth by those who foresaw the danger. They pointed out the impossibility of traveling on Long Island even if they should reach the shore. They had nothing to take with them to satisfy nature, and without nourishment they could not subsist, and to apply for it was sure detection.

Notwithstanding all those arguments, there were a few resolutely bent to make the trial. "We must die here," say they, "and we can do no more in the attempt," and [when] a suitable time (in their opinion) arrived, the hole was opened at about 12 o'clock of a dark, rainy night, and four from among us were assisted by [us in] securing clothes just sufficient to cover their nakedness if they should be so fortunate as to reach the shore. This was done by tying them upon the shoulders, [they being] otherwise naked. Four of them by assistance got into the water and waited till all had gotten in as was previously agreed upon by them. They set off for the shore, which was not more than a quarter of a mile distant.

It appeared that our guard had long been acquainted with our intentions and kept a good lookout for their murderous purpose [of] having a feast in slaughter among the victims. A boat was ready in waiting under the ship's quarter with the rowers and bloodthirsty soldiers, and having ascertained that no more were likely to descend into the water, they then pursued those who had already put off, which were easily seen by the sparkling of the water, an effect which a stormy night always produces upon the water. Report of a gun was soon heard succeeded by several other reports, and the prisoners that were then in the water were distinctly heard from the hole to cry for mercy, but the darkness of the night prevented our seeing the massacre from our situation, but we knew the event would be attended with murder, for

> *Wounds are their sport, as ruin is their aim;*
> *On their dark souls compassion has no claim.*
> [Freneau]

Massacre

The prisoners became much agitated in consequence of the firing upon those who had gotten out, for the report had run throughout the ship almost instantly, and it was not long before the gratings were unlaid and the soldiers with their lanterns assisted in bringing down between decks a naked and bleeding man whose naked and bleeding body they placed in a bunk and for this time left a piece of candle and ascended the deck and secured the grating. This circumstance reached us in the gun room, and knowing it to be one of our late comrades, we fought, some of us, our way to the place where he lay and immediately discovered it to be Mr. Lawrence.

His arm was nearly separated from his body by the stroke of a cutlass, and [he was] otherwise wounded. This barbarous transaction was inflicted, he said, after his hand was on the

43

Massacre

The narrative page for "Massacre." (*Rhode Island Historical Society*)

gunwale of the boat, there imploring their forbearance. His distressed condition would not then admit of our asking him any questions in regard to the fate of the others. He once asked where Nelson was (one of the adventurers), which was all he ever said on the subject, nor did we ever after hear from them, but in all probability they were everyone murdered in the water.

> *On the hard floor his bleeding body lay;*
> *No kind assistance then could we convey.*
> *The glimmering light affords the scanty means*
> *With hearts of grief to view the dreadful scene.*

This was the only time that I had ever seen a light below, and the effect was horrid beyond description. This event had disturbed the slumbers of the night and curiosity had induced many to surround the bunk where he lay. We lamented the condition of our fellow prisoner and regretted that we could afford him no surgical aid. His wounds were bound up as well as we could do it, and a shirt and a pair of trousers were also furnished him and his head bound up in a handkerchief. It seemed as though the whole mass of blood had flowed from his body and still adhered to him and his clotted hair. We had not even the means to wash his body that night. We had seen many die, and death had now become familiar to us, but to see a fellow mortal thus linger in misery and not excite the compassion of those who had just inflicted the wound, and [to see him] die for the want of surgical aid was to us distressing indeed.

> *On every side dire objects met the sight,*
> *The pallid forms, and murders of the night,*
> *//*
> *There no soft voice their bitter fate bemoan'd*
> *And [blood flow'd freely] while the victim groan'd.*
> [Freneau]

There was no surgical aid whatever afforded to this object of compassion. It was indeed promised but never came. The prisoners very humanely rendered him every assistance that their feeble means would admit of. They washed his body and dressed his wound as well as they could, but a mortification took place, and the poor man died in a state of delirium.

> *Some struck with madness, some with scurvy pain'd,*
> *But still of putrid fevers most complain'd!*
> [Freneau]

There was never an inquiry even made by our foes about this wounded man, and I presume that he was left to suffer in the manner he did as an example of terror, in order to deter us from an attempt of the kind by cutting out. We were never reprimanded for the transaction. The hole was again planked up and perfectly secured, and no attempt of the kind took place [again] while I was there.

It was needless [useless] to endeavor to escape by finding our way upon Long Island. They had quartered upon the island several regiments. Among the rest was a regiment of refugees. They were very vigilant in the cause of their royal master and took delight in apprehending us and replacing us in confinement.

> *No age, no sex from lust and murder free,*
> *And, black as night, the hell born refugee!*
> *//*
> *And every wretch whom honour should detest*
> *There finds a home–and [Benedict] Arnold with the rest.*
> [Freneau]

It was always in our power to have knocked their guards in [the] head and have them overboard by day, but this would have answered no purpose. Escape upon Long Island was to no purpose for the reason before mentioned, though I knew several instances when it was effected, [once] in particular by one of my shipmates in the *Chance* (James Pitcher). He was put upon the sick list and conveyed to Blackwell's Island [renamed Welfare Island between 1921 and 1973 and subsequently Roosevelt Island] from which he got to Long Island and by due precaution passed the sound and got home and is now at the time of my writing one of the three survivors only remaining of that crew.[56]

56. Dring takes a very pessimistic view of the possibilities of escape from the *Jersey,* despite his own successful escape from the *Good Hope* and his personal knowledge of James Pitcher's escape. Fleeing the prison was obviously a desperate action with long odds of success. Compared with the great number of prisoners, few actually attempted it, and even fewer succeeded. Yet among the extant prisoner narratives can be found some exciting stories of successful escape. See, for instance, *Adventures of Christopher Hawkins,* 47, 76; *Adventures of Ebenezer Fox,* 147; Andros, *Old Jersey Captive,* 14; *Memorandum* by Roswell Palmer, concerning his uncle's two escapes, and letter by William Pitt Palmer, Roswell's son, to Henry T. Drowne, April 15, 1865, describing his father's escape, both in Dawson's appendix, Dring-Greene, *Recollections,* 174–80; statement by Jonathan Manley dated September 1, 1845, printed in Onderdonk, *Revolutionary Incidents,* 236–37. Jeremiah Johnson, who lived as a boy during the war on the Wallabout shore, states that the percentage of successful escapes was high, and that the equivalent of an underground railroad of friendly Long Islanders helped prisoners escape to New England. He also describes a daring escape by rowboat all the way to the Connecticut shore (*Recollections of Brooklyn and New York,* printed in Dawson's appendix, 190–91). Escape was possible from the other prisons at New York as well. Dr. Elias Cornelius, for example, simply walked out of a hospital prison located in a church three days after he had been transferred there from the Sugar House (*Journal of Dr. Elias,* 10–13). Escape attempts were frequent in the English prisons as well. Most were group escapes (in one example more than one hundred escaped) following the digging of a tunnel under the wall. These tunnels were constantly being dug and the loose dirt concealed in chests, chimneys, etc. Many holes were discovered before they were finished, but some fulfilled their purpose. For those caught while digging or after they had escaped, the standard treatment in both English prisons was forty days in the Black Hole, a separate dungeon, with one-half the normal allowance. See the sources listed in note 19 to the editor's introduction.

But to return to our situation on board the *Jersey* after the massacre of the night, we were kept below by way of punishment until about 10 o'clock the next day. This produced the natural complaint of heat and thirst with all the aggravating effect which it then produced. As before mentioned, this mode of punishment was frequently adopted by them upon the most trifling occurrence.[57]

> *By planks and ponderous beams completely wall'd,*
> *In vain for water, and in vain, [we] call'd–*
> //
> *Where cruel thirst the parching throat invades,*
> *Dries up the man, and fits him for the shades.*
> [Freneau]

The Prisoners' Petition [to General Washington]

Our numbers were daily increasing on board the *Jersey* notwithstanding the great mortality among us, which now raged to an unprecedented degree [with] no prospect whatever for any exchange. Our situation now became deplorable indeed, and we were all filled with dismay. Under those dreadful circumstances it was thought advisable to represent if possible to General Washington our deplorable situation and implore his interference on our behalf. But previous to addressing him it was necessary to have permission so to do, and for this purpose we drew up a petition to [Sir Henry] Clinton, then commander at New York, stating to him our desire of seeking some relief from our deplorable situation by addressing General Washington upon the subject of our captivity, which petition should be examined, and if approved of, we further asked the favor of sending a messenger from among our number, and the commissary of prisoners (in this case) assisted us

57. The only other time Dring mentions this mode of punishment is after the July 4 atrocities, which he certainly did not consider a trifling occurrence (see pages 75–78).

in making the communication to the British commander and finally in obtaining his permission for three men whom we might think proper to select from among us [who] should be furnished with a passport immediately to proceed on the embassy. We lost no time in making the choice of our men, and I had the satisfaction to find that our late commander (Captain Aborn) and our doctor, Mr. Joseph Bowen, composed two out of the three who were to proceed on this business.[58]

Our petition [was] drawn up and the letter of introduction handed to the committee of embassy. The address was signed by another committee from among the prisoners and signed by them in the behalf of the whole. This address to General Washington stated to him our motive in writing him upon a subject which we conceived he had no agency. Yet such was our deplorable situation that we had flattered ourselves it would meet, when duly represented, his attention and that our sufferings might induce him to use his influence in our behalf. We knew that soldiers had never been exchanged for sailors in [any] case and that his concerns did not extend to navy departments. Yet it might be in his power to have our sufferings mitigated even if an exchange could not be effected. We requested that the representation of our committee who would have the pleasure of visiting him might have its weight, as they could relate such matters as we could not commit to paper. The committee was empowered to make a tender of our services as soldiers or any way that they might be serviceable dur-

58. Concerning Captain Aborn, see note 12. Joseph Bowen, the *Chance's* doctor, came from a branch of this prominent Rhode Island family, which includes several generations of physicians. The son of Dr. Benjamin Bowen of Providence, he was born in 1755 or 1756. In December 1782, not long after his imprisonment, he married Hannah Simons. They settled in Providence, where he practiced medicine until his death in 1832 (*Representative Men and Old Families of Rhode Island. . . .* (Chicago: J. H. Beers, 1908), 1011). See also note 64. It appears from the documents that if a third member of the petitioning embassy was selected, he did not make the trip.

ing the war, upon condition of release. This, however, was a verbal message, as it would not have done to have committed this proposition to writing for obvious reasons well known to the reader.[59]

Everything being ready for the departure of our committee, they were once more instructed to represent (verbally) our crowded situation, our scanty fare, the badness of our provisions, our putrid water and wormy bread, and the dreadful mortality which prevailed among us, all of which they promised to relate. We wished them success in our behalf, and they departed upon their errand from the old *Jersey* undoubtedly with joy. We almost envied them their happiness upon this occasion.

It was with the greatest anxiety that we awaited the return of our committee. Alternate hopes and fears succeeded [each other], and our whole minds were for some days taken up with the thoughts of the result. We in particular from the New England states [were] persuaded that something favorable would proceed from this representation. At any rate, we had this consolation, that our condition could not be worsened.

I here have said that we from New England seemed to feel ourselves most interested in this application, for among us there certainly were many who did not even know that such a proposition was in contemplation. I mean the foreigners and those who had been long on board and had given up all expectation of any release until death should effect it and [who] really appeared to me to be quite indifferent as to their fate or accustomed to their long sufferings. But undoubtedly a release

59. The prisoners seem to have had a fairly clear idea of the difficulties involved in their being exchanged. Their only real hope was to persuade General Washington to accept David Sproat's proposal to exchange American privateersmen for British soldiers. But Washington's mind could not be changed on this matter. See page xxviii and note 27 to the editor's introduction.

would have appeared like a resurrection from the dead to those miserable and neglected men there at this time.

> *[A thousand] wretches here, denied all light,*
> *In crowded mansions pass the infernal night,*
> *//*
> *Shut from the blessings of the evening air,*
> *Pensive we lay with mingled corpses there.*
> [Freneau]

After a few days absence our committee returned to New York and brought the reply from General Washington directed to the committee who signed the petition in behalf of the prisoners. After perusing it themselves, the prisoners were all summoned upon the spar deck to hear the reply to our petition, the purport of which was that he had received our letter upon the subject of our complaints and that he had listened to the representation given by our committee with sentiments of commiseration and due concern that our sufferings and the causes had been duly related by those whom we had appointed for this purpose, which was lamentable to hear, and although the application to him was (as we had observed in our letter) made on mistaken grounds as he had no agency in this business, but conceiving our application to him was the result of our forlorn condition, he should do all in his power to mitigate our sufferings, and the cause should be investigated and our complaints be said before Congress.

He told the committee (verbally and very justly) that our sufferings by detention were in consequence of the total neglect of securing the British prisoners (taken at sea) for the purpose of exchange, observing that a large proportion of the prisoners were taken in private armed vessels not of the United States service and that it had been a custom among them (as he understood) for the sailors to enter on board immediately after capture. At any rate, they were in all cases at liberty to go where they pleased when [they] arrived [at port]. The owners or captors did not wish to be at the expense of their maintenance, the town or state where they were carried had no disposition to be at the cost of their support or confinement, and the general government only took cognizance of such prisoners as were made by the vessels really in the service of the United States. To those circumstances he attributed our detention, as there were not numbers of prisoners obtained to answer the purpose of exchange, which remarks were founded in truth and are here related to show the cause. However, he would write to the commander in chief of the British at New York upon the subject of our complaint, and if our release or exchange could not be immediately effected, he hoped that our sufferings would be in some measure mitigated by a removal from those infectious ships and that our diet might be of a better quality etc.

The copy of the letter to General Clinton was read to us and another to the commissary of prisoners also. The purport of those letters was much the same. It was a repetition of our complaints to him setting forth our then crowded conditions and ill treatment etc. He expressed a great desire that our sufferings might be mitigated by enlargement [of our space] and [asked] if it was absolutely necessary that we should be confined on board of ships. He requested that clean ships might be procured for our accommodation and the preservation of our health. He observed that our principal complaints arose from our crowded situation and unwholesome diet and that if the British prisoners in our possession were placed in the same situation, it would in all probability produce among them the same effect, and putrid contagions would be the result among them. He requested them upon the principle of humanity to redress our grievances and hoped that some arrangement might be made whereby a general exchange of prisoners might be effected and a total liberation of those unfortunate men be accomplished, and to produce this much desired event, nothing on his part should be wanting to produce it without delay, and he hoped that the present communication between them upon this subject would eventually lead to that termination and gladden the hearts of the prisoners by the joy of returning to their anxious families.

This was to the best of my present recollection the purport of those letters, all of which were published in the newspapers of that time, and I regret that one could not be now found which contained them, but they made an impression upon my mind (like other scenes on board the *Jersey* which cannot be forgotten and are nearly the purport, as before stated in the above narration).[60]

Our committee did not return among us as prisoners on board, but for their services were paroled upon Long Island (at Flatbush), and shortly after, they had their paroles extended so far as to return home to their families.[61]

60. Dring's information here is quite detailed and accurate. He probably was familiar with all the relevant documents printed in Dawson's appendix, Dring-Greene, *Recollections*, 138–42, which includes only one Washington letter, to Rear Admiral Digby, dated June 5, 1782. The date is significant, for it shows that, contrary to Dring's general chronological ordering, these events precede the fourth of July. Knowing this helps disprove Dring's contention that he was finally exchanged in October after almost five months on the *Jersey*. See note 71.

61. Parole of privateer captains (and most high-ranking army officers) was apparently a fairly common practice. Most were housed with loyalist families on Long Island. See, for instance, an entry in Ford, *Samuel Blackley Webb*, 2:99. Others, as in Dring's description here, managed to get paroled home. Another example of this, under different circumstances, is the case of William Drowne, who, being ill, was at least once allowed to leave the *Jersey* for an extended period to live at home in Newport. There, and later back on the *Jersey*, his brother, Dr. Solomon Drowne, cared for him. He never recovered, however, and died in 1786. See documents and letters printed in Dawson's appendix, Dring-Greene, *Recollections*, 162–73, and Dandridge, *American Prisoners*, 433–39.

It may be necessary to just mention that Captain Collins had been paroled ever since our arrival in New York and now returned with the before mentioned. When he was captured he had a deck load of livestock, which was very acceptable to the captors, more so than cannon and men. His liberation was doubtless effected from this circumstance.[62]

We shortly after found that our remonstrance to General Washington was attended with some benefit, at least we attributed a change in our diet for the better to that circumstance. We received bread of a better quality and drew butter in lieu of [the] oil which had been served out to us and [was] so rank that we could not even endure the smell of it, as before mentioned. We also had an awning furnished us, a very desirable thing to us, as before,

> No friendly awning cast a welcome shade,
> Once it was promis'd, and was never made.
> [Freneau]

We had now the benefit of this awning and a wind sail to conduct the fresh air down between decks by day, and it was to be lamented that indulgence could not be extended to the night when it was most wanted, but the hatches or gratings must be laid at all events, and of course the wind sail could not be conducted below for fear (as I suppose) that the prisoners might make their escape by means of it, but of this they need not have been under any apprehensions, situated as we were, but to this and every other privation we were obliged to submit and to flatter ourselves that the little change which we had for a few days past for the better would finally lead to some event more favorable to our condition, though from the mortality which still prevailed, there could be no alleviation but by the interposition of divine Providence or a removal from the contagion itself, of which we could have little or no hope.

62. See note 16.

Captain Aborn Returns Home [and Prospects for an Exchange]

When our captain (Aborn) had obtained his parole home (from Long Island), he wrote us word of his liberation and that he should, previous to his leaving New York, pay us a short visit and endeavor to ascertain the condition of the crew that was captured with him and requested our first officer, Mr. John Tillinghast,[63] to have a list of the deceased and also of the survivors and where they were at the time, that is, all on board the *Jersey* and those who might be in the hospital ships or elsewhere, and also requested that it might be made known on board to the prisoners that they might avail themselves of this opportunity of writing their friends if they felt disposed so to do, which he or his companions would take charge of. All of us (at least those in the gun room) were employed in writing to our friends, and such of the sailors as had the means or the inclination did the same. Our letters were always subject to an inspection previous to their being sent off, but in this instance they underwent no examination whatever, and we were sorry that we did not mention our ill treatment more fully, which was omitted under the apprehensions of being stopped on that account.

Captain Aborn came on board the next day accompanied by seven others who were paroled with him to return home, but they came no nearer to us than the head of the gangway ladder and passed through the barricade door upon the quarterdeck. Precaution, I suppose, induced them to keep thus distant (they were undoubtedly more likely to take the prevailing fever than those who resided on board), or [there was some] other motive they had for keeping aloof from those they knew and who were all striving to speak to them previous to their

63. John Tillinghast belonged to one of the oldest and most prominent Rhode Island families. He was born probably on December 9, 1743, the son of Elisha and Deliverance Tillinghast of Providence, and died May 6, 1810 (*Representative Men*, 1665).

leaving us but were sadly disappointed. The prisoners, however, had all their letters received with assurances of the best endeavors of Captain Aborn to effect our speedy relief. He requested that it might be made known generally to the prisoners that their condition would be fully and justly represented upon his return home, and to those who were captured with him, he promised to use his exertions for our exchange and assured us if so many British prisoners could be found, no money should prevent their being procured and sent on for the purpose of our exchange, and if this could not be effected, we might expect that some clothing and necessaries should be sent us, and [he] recommended to us to keep up our spirits etc. This communication was made to our first officer, Mr. John Tillinghast, as before stated, who had then an interview with Captain Aborn upon the quarterdeck, and the purport was made known to us from Mr. Tillinghast and was in substance what I have here related.[64]

64. This visit by Aborn, prior to his parole, is interesting in view of a controversial document which he, Joseph Bowen, Captain Charles Collins, and ten other privateer captains signed on June 22, 1782. The document is allegedly the report of a subcommittee of this group (including Collins but not Aborn or Bowen) concerning conditions on the *Jersey* and other prison ships as observed during an inspection tour just completed with David Sproat and George Rutherford, surgeon to the hospital ships. The report gives a relatively rosy picture of conditions and of the policies of Sproat and Rutherford, a picture quite at variance with all other American descriptions of the prison ships. Within a few days of the signing of the report, Sproat had had it printed in the *New York Royal Gazette* (June 26, 1782), and the signers had all been paroled home. Although Aborn was not a member of the inspection subcommittee, his visit to the *Jersey*, described by Dring, probably happened at about the same time, and the seven other captains who came with Aborn must have been part of the group of thirteen. It is significant that Dring states that Aborn and the others did not mingle with the prisoners, but kept to the crew's end of the ship, where Aborn did have an interview with John Tillinghast. Nor does Dring mention any other officers coming among them for an inspection. A prisoner named John Cochran later signed an affidavit on July16, 1782, printed in the *Philadelphia Pennsylvania Packet* on September

About this time some of the sick were put on Blackwell's Island. This was considered by those who had that indulgence to be a great favor and we envied them their happiness although they were sick. I made an attempt to obtain this favor by a pretended complaint but could not succeed, which finally was a happy circumstance for me, as will hereafter appear.

> "We, too, grown weary of that horrid shade,
> "Petitioned early for the doctor's aid;
> "his aid denied, more deadly symptoms came,
> "Weak, and yet weaker, glow'd the vital flame;"
> And when disease had worn us down so low
> "That few could tell if we were ghosts or no."
> [Freneau]

10, 1782) in which he states that he saw the inspection group come on board the *Jersey*, go immediately to the crew's end of the ship, and never inspect the ship or talk with the prisoners. He also refutes the subcommittee's positive report of conditions as false. Americans quickly concluded that the captains had been blackmailed into signing the false report in order to obtain parole. This may be accurate, but Aborn, at least, may have felt he had a compelling reason to justify perjuring himself. He had just journeyed to speak personally with General Washington about the possibilities of exchanging the *Jersey* prisoners through government channels. He must have returned without much hope of success in that direction (see page xxviii to the editor's introduction). His only alternative was somehow to get home to Providence in order to arouse people there to initiate a private exchange. This was Aborn's stated purpose in obtaining parole, and to this end he apparently was willing to sign a document he must have known was false. The relevant documents are printed in Dawson's appendix, Dring-Greene, *Recollections*, 143–57. An alternative scenario suggests that the entire exchange of the *Chance's* crew was a publicity stunt engineered by David Sproat to bolster royalist support. In this scenario, the signatures on the controversial inspection document were coerced in exchange for the parole of the captains and doctor. See Burrows, *Forgotten Patriots*, 183–87.

By the removal of the sick our room between decks became more comfortable. The sick bunks were in part taken away and the sick removed as soon as their condition was made known. This afforded us great relief on many accounts, and our place of confinement [was] considerably enlarged by this circumstance, though the mortality no way abated. The weather [was] extremely warm by day and by night scarcely to be endured, but hope all-cheering kept us alive. It was near the setting sun while we were, some of us, flattering ourselves that a few days might produce something in our favor. Our situation, we knew, must then be known to our friends in Providence, and we did not doubt the exertion of Captain Aborn to effect our exchange.

We at this moment discovered the white flag from the masthead of a sloop and at once discovered her to be a cartel,[65] but she did not approach us so near as to now ascertain anything further for this night. We were soon turned below as usual, but the night was spent by many of us in the greatest anxiety, in a particular manner by the survivors of the *Chance's* crew. We had been long expecting a cartel, though in reality we could have no foundation for such an event further than our great desire. We observed from the direction from which we saw her make her appearance that she was undoubtedly from some of the New England states, and to such of the prisoners as belonged in that section, the prospect was cheering, and it was truly a long night to us. We had worked up our imagination to a great degree, and soon as we were upon deck in the morning, every eye was fixed upon the cartel, and we saw that her deck was full of men which we supposed were British prisoners. We saw them soon after disembark from the cartel and proceed toward New York in the commissary's boat, but we

65. A cartel is a written agreement for the exchange of prisoners of war. A ship used for the physical exchange of prisoners also was commonly referred to as a cartel.

still knew not from whence she came nor whose happiness it would be to be benefited by this so desirable an event.

The Exchange

It was not until the afternoon of this day that we observed a boat now approaching us from the cartel, for we had watched every movement from her and were impatient to know our fate, and as the [boat] neared us, we saw the commissary of prisoners on board, and to our great joy, we now saw our well known townsman, Captain William Corey.[66] All of us from Providence were now in full expectation that our captivity was now nearly to an end, which happy event was soon verified by its being known that the cartel was from Providence and their object was to effect the exchange of the crew of the *Chance*, that is, as far as their number of English prisoners would effect it, and that the number they brought was forty, fully sufficient to exchange every survivor of that crew, at least all that were then on board the *Jersey*.

We had no opportunity to ask any questions of Captain Corey, nor did we require it at that time and courted a most favorable opportunity. It may be readily supposed we were all ready to answer to the summons of our names, and such things as we intended to take with us were ready packed up and in our hands. We knew that there would be no second call nor any delay whatever, and our eyes were upon the stretch and our mouths ready to answer "here." The ceremony was as follows. The commissary and Captain Corey were upon the quarterdeck, and Mr. Tillinghast, our first officer, was directed to say if the man who answered to the name called was one of the crew of the *Chance*. If in the affirmative, he was ordered to

66. Captain William Corey, from yet another prominent Providence family, was himself involved in privateering, on the *Phoenix*, in 1782.

descend immediately into the boat (then in waiting) at the bottom of the ladder.

I had previous to this my clothes ready packed up in a bag (for we were not allowed to take away any chest by the regulations among the prisoners) and even disposed of my cleft of wood before mentioned, which I considered of great value to the possessors. This I disposed of by legacy upon condition of my being exchanged [with] some other effects in the same way, as was customary, such as tin kettle, etc.

We had all ascended the deck and placed ourselves as near the barricade door as possible, waiting with anxiety to hear our names called. Our hearts beat hard with joy, fear, and apprehensions at the same time. Our first officer, John Tillinghast, was the first upon the list and [was] detained to certify to the rest of us as being the same called, as before stated. There was no delay, nor was there any required. My name was soon called, and I cheerily answered "here." The commissary pointed to the boat. I believe I never stepped quicker. It certainly was to me the most happy moment that I had ever experienced in all my life.

I even viewed the commissary with a degree of complacency at this time, though we all held him in detestation. I even bestowed upon him a bow as I passed (for which heaven forgive me) and descended the ladder with emotions I had never known nor can I describe, and when I had gotten into the boat, I could not refrain from shedding a tear of joy, and I saw with pleasure my former shipmates descend the ladder one after another, but not a word escaped our lips by way of any congratulations upon the event. Fears and apprehensions still dwelt upon our minds. We could scarcely be made to believe that we were then without the limits of the *Jersey*.

It was an unfortunate circumstance that some of our crew were then on board the hospital ships or upon Blackwell's Island sick, as they could not be benefited by the present exchange. There was none among us to urge the necessity of seeking after those poor, neglected victims. Self is generally at the bottom of all our concerns, particularly so in our present situation, and they were abandoned to their fate by being left behind.[67] Delays were considered dangerous and dreaded by us, and the sick were considered as an encumbrance to us and dangerous companions, and they were not even mentioned (that I know of) and certainly not sought after, though we, many of us, regretted their absence. Having now as many on board the boat as she would carry at one time, we put off from the old *Jersey* and soon arrived on board the cartel to our unspeakable joy.

> *Some tears we shed for the remaining crew,*
> *Then curs'd the hulk, and from her sides withdrew.*
> [Freneau]

[Having] now gotten upon the deck of the cartel, I could scarcely bring my mind to realize that I was quit of the *Jersey*. Fears from unforeseen events which might still detain us dwelt upon our minds and in some measure had a tendency to dampen our happiness. The very thought of again being put on board the hulk was terrifying to us, and I believe that an event of this kind would have been immediate death to most of us.

It was with pleasure that we received our next boatload on board the cartel, which completed the whole number of the crew of the *Chance*, which was thirty-five. The residue was either dead or otherwise separated from us at the time of this

67. According to the *Providence Gazette*, July 27, 1782, eight of the *Chance's* crew were left because they were ill. Dring also left hundreds of others behind on the *Jersey* and on the hospital ships. Although other private exchanges brought the release of many prisoners, the Americans and British never did reach agreement on a general exchange, and thus many prisoners were still incarcerated when peace was declared in April 1783, at which time they all finally were released.

exchange.[68] But we had several among us who had answered or assumed the names of some of our deceased crew. Those were officers from the gun room in sailor's dress, and they passed by the assent of Mr. Tillinghast, as before mentioned, as he knew the whole number of forty could not be found on board the *Jersey*, and as the deficiency in number, say five, was not present and would not be sought after at that time, there was no impropriety of someone else then being benefited by this circumstance, and their assuming the names of the deceased was a concerted plan which so far succeeded. It was well known that had there been more of our crew then on board the *Jersey* than the number of British prisoners sent for our release, say forty, not one more would have been permitted to depart, and the unfortunate number would have been those on the bottom of the list. This circumstance to them would have been dreadful indeed, even worse than to those whose absence precluded them from the exchange. I must here observe that our foes, like the Algerians, put a value upon our emaciated bodies.

It was near sunset before the transportation of the prisoners was fully effected and when completed, the commissary left

68. If we add Aborn and Bowen to Dring's thirty-five, we account for 37 out of an original 65. This leaves 28, representing a mortality/sickness rate of 43 percent in two months. According to "a merchant" writing in the *Providence Gazette*, July 27, 1782, the *Chance's* crew originally numbered only fifty-seven, and only twenty-five came home on the cartel. He describes the fates of the others as follows: Captain Aborn was paroled; one joined the British navy; one escaped from the prize ship; one was detained in New York; one was exchanged from a hospital ship early in July, when he was close to death; one each was exchanged to New London and Boston; eight were left behind by the Providence cartel due to illness; and seventeen died at New York. Twenty-six out of 57 represents a 46 percent mortality/sickness rate. The merchant furthermore states that only three or four of the lucky 25 who returned on the cartel were healthy enough to walk off the ship in Providence.

the cartel, we all hoped for the last time, and prayed it might be the last time that we should ever see his frightful face. I now cast my eyes toward the dismal hulk. She appeared with more horror than ever, [with] the sun in its horizontal position striking upon her filthy side and the then moving multitude in motion upon the spar deck and forecastle about to be turned below for the night, probably to many for the last time, never to ascend the deck again or view another sun. I must here confess that my soul melted with compassion toward those most miserable beings. While I was among them and in their present situation, perhaps I thought less of their or my own condition than I now did, who though only a spectator, knew well by sorrowful and sad experience of nearly five months what they had to endure and the scene they had to pass, not only for that night, but while they were numbered among the living in this sink of all human misery.

My God, what a contrast with us who were then congratulating each other upon this happy event. We were overwhelmed with raptures and intoxicated with joy, figuring to ourselves the all-cheering prospect that another day would probably produce the happy time when we should be entirely free and beyond the limits of our detested foe, and every surrounding object would be seen with pleasure, our greedy eyes stretched to discover some well known spire as we passed along the happy shores of old Connecticut on our way to Rhode Island, and at present

> *No sentries stand to guard the midnight post,*
> *Nor lay the hatches on a crowd of host.*

We now had the pleasure to view the setting sun and the approaching evening, and no insulting voice greeted our ears with the usual salutation of "Down, rebels, down." We soon had the pleasure to see a lighted candle, which we had not seen for several months (except on the murderous occasion before mentioned). Every object and change contributed to our joy. We were at liberty to pass the night as we pleased. This was a pleasure indeed to us who had never seen the stars in their zenith for several months and only viewed them in their horizontal positions, and that through the iron gratings of our prison. This indulgence to us was exquisite and was duly enjoyed by us throughout this happy night long to be remembered by the survivors.

It was on this happy occasion, when I had no inclination to sleep, that I learned the means of our liberation (or exchange) from Captain Gladding of Bristol, who owned and then commanded the sloop were on board of.[69] It seems that upon the return of our Captain Aborn to Providence, our deplorable situation on board the *Jersey* became generally known and commiserated. Our respectable owners, Messrs. Clark and Nightingale of Providence, used (with our other friends) every exertion to effect our exchange, which was attended with very considerable expense, but the advances were made, and forty British prisoners were found in Boston, which were marched up to Providence where the sloop was chartered of Captain Gladding of Bristol to proceed to New York with the prisoners for the sole purpose of effecting our exchange, that is, as far as their numbers would effect, and Captain William Corey of Providence was employed to take charge of the prisoners and effect the exchange, for which he had the necessary documents.[70] The cartel was well ballasted with water and plenty of good provisions for the British prisoners and ourselves and arrived safe at New York at the time I have mentioned, though

69. The Gladding family of Bristol is both prominent and voluminous. Which of several Captain Gladdings this is remains unclear.

70. In the process of arranging these private exchanges, the British prisoners were subjected to a strange kind of buying and selling akin to slavery. This is an interesting case of private enterprise stepping in to fulfill a role usually performed by government, as indeed was the practice of commercial firms chartering privateers in the first place.

I do not recollect the date but think it was early in the month of October 1782.[71]

I must not here omit the exertions made by our then fellow citizen, Captain John Creed, who was at that time deputy commissary of prisoners, and by his exertions, I have been told, we were much indebted for our deliverance from captivity and of course for our lives.

71. Dring has clearly overestimated the length of time he spent on the *Jersey*. He correctly stated above that he was captured in May. He arrived on the *Jersey* on May 19 (*New-York Gazette and Weekly Mercury*, May 20, 1782, *New York Royal Gazette*, May 22, 1782, both printed in Dawson's note in Dring-Greene, *Recollections*, 25; *Providence Gazette*, July 27, 1782). But he incorrectly estimated his imprisonment to have lasted almost five months. This apparently led him to the October date (which happens to be the same month he escaped from the *Good Hope* in 1779). Actually he was exchanged in July, only two weeks after the July 4 incidents. Aborn and Bowen visited Washington shortly before June 5, 1782, within two weeks of their capture (see note 60). By June 22 Aborn was about to go home to Providence to arrange the exchange (see note 64). Dring correctly estimates the time from Aborn's departure to the cartel's arrival to be fairly short. Actually, the exchange of the *Chance's* crew appears to have been one in a series of private exchanges involving 249 prisoners over a twelve-day period preceding July 17. Besides the 40 going to Providence, 102 went to Boston, 84 to New London, and 23 to Baltimore (*New York Royal Gazette*, July 17, 1782, printed in Dawson's note in Dring-Greene, *Recollections*, 111). The *Providence Gazette* on July 27, 1782, printed information both supporting and contradicting Dring. There is a notice of a cartel's arrival on July 21 with 39 former prisoners, a fortieth having died on the way into Providence. There is also a death notice for Winchester Bicknell dated July 20. Finally, there is a letter from "a merchant" stating that only 25 of the *Chance's* crew of 57 arrived in the cartel, on July 22, after having left New York on July 20 (see note 68). It may be that the cartel arrived during the evening (in agreement with Dring's recollection) of July 21, and that the former prisoners disembarked on the morning of July 22. However, that fails to explain Bicknell's reported death on July 20. In any case, the arrival date can with certainty be fixed within a period of two days. This shows that Dring actually was on the *Jersey* for just over two months from May 19 to July 20, 1782.

But to return to the cartel, we found no letters, and Captain Corey being onshore at New York, we could not get any tidings from our friends in Providence, as the captain of the cartel and his men did not belong there, as before mentioned, but the night was spent cheerfully, and our eyes greeted the white flag that was still flying.

Leaving New York

The morning arose with joyful prospects, different indeed from what we had been long accustomed to, yet [it] presented to our sad view the disgusting hulk of the *Jersey* and the deadly appearance of the odious hospital ships around her. We could not lose sight of the sufferings of those who were now ascending the deck. We were too far off to distinguish them personally but recollected our messmates to whom we had become endeared by our mutual captivity and all its accumulated horrors. And while our wholesome and abundant breakfast was then preparing, it could but bring to our minds the condition of our truly lamented late companions and bring fresh to mind every privation we had endured and the provisions we [there] received compared to what we now saw before us and gladly would have relinquished this morning if [the prisoners] could have been benefited by the donation.

> *Once [on a time] we try'd to move our flinty chief,*
> *And thus address'd him, holding up the beef:*
> *"See [steward], see! what rotten bones we pick,*
> *"What kills the healthy cannot cure the sick:*
> *"Not dogs on such by Christian men are fed,*
> *"And see, good [steward], see, what lousy bread!"*
> *//*
> *"Out of my sight!"—nor more he deign'd to say,*
> *But whisk'd about, and frowning, strode away.*
> [Freneau]

But we now had all partaken [of] a good breakfast, and in good season we found that it had a wonderful effect upon us, and we began to think and feel that we once more were men. The time passed tediously waiting for the arrival of Captain Corey. We were anxious to trip the anchor. At last the boat conveying him appeared. It was about 10 o'clock when he got on board and gave directions to get underway. The anchor was run up to the bow by the prisoners. [We] required no windlass or capstan for this purpose at this time. Our sail was instantly set. Our stern, to our joy, turned toward the *Jersey*, a circumstance which we had long contemplated and now happily realized. With a free wind and favorable tide, we soon lost sight of the disgusting hulk, the old *Jersey*, and the other equally disgusting objects at the Wallabout, in particular the much dreaded sand bank, the depot of the fallen victims who had paid the debt of nature in their country's cause by the cruel hands of a vindictive foe.

> *Ah! come the day when from this bloody shore*
> *Fate shall remove them to return no more—*
> [Freneau]

On our progress along Hell Gate, etc., we had to pass very near the shore of Blackwell's Island, where some of the sick had been placed, among which were at that time several of our former crew, convalescent. Those men knew the cartel had come from Providence, the object of which was to exchange the crew of the *Chance*, and as such they flattered themselves that they should be taken on board, and to prevent delay they had all then assembled upon the shore with their bundles in their hands. But to their then unspeakable grief and horrid disappointment, they saw us pass along and show no disposition to stop to take them on board. We knew them and lamented the necessity of leaving them, but we had no agency in the present transaction and could only wave the hand, to which salutation, however, they made no return and remained as long as we could see them like statues fixed to the earth and unmovable.

The reader may judge of their grief and disappointment upon this occasion, those neglected men. I have since seen one of that number. He observed that their removal from the *Jersey* had been attended with a wonderful effect by being placed upon the island [and] that they had been exulting in the change for the better, but to meet this dreadful disappointment caused them to regret the removal. They now viewed their situation as forlorn, as in all probability they should be soon again conveyed on board the *Jersey* as well men, there to undergo a second death. (This one, however, made his escape.)

We had still two guard ships of the enemy to pass for examination. We, however, met no detention on this score, and when we had gotten entirely clear of them, and all fear and apprehensions of detention had subsided as to our enemies, we then gave loose to our general joy and congratulations. We seemed to breathe another air. It was the air of freedom, which we inhaled with rapture, and every countenance bespoke the happy change. Our hearts beat with pleasing expectation, and our progress along the land of liberty was every moment presenting to our view some new and well known object where dwelt harmony and peace. Under such circumstances, who could but be happy, particularly as we reflected upon our escape from death while on board the hulk, but I will here renounce the odious name and hope I may not have occasion to even mention it while dwelling upon this my narrative. The name of the *Jersey* is disgusting, and to those who have been within her putrefied bowels [it] is terrifying to the recollection, yet durable to the memory.

> *[No] soldiers sent to guard us on our road,*
> *Joyful we left the [Jersey's] dire abode.*
> [Freneau]

Passage Home and Occurrences

Several of the crew were unwell when they entered on board the cartel, and the change of air and diet produced several new cases of the fever, a fever which we had long been accustomed to during our confinement and the consequences, as before stated. We, however, lost none on board the cartel, as our passage was only two days. We attributed our present sickness to the partaking too freely of fish and vegetables, both of which we had in the greatest abundance and to neither of which we had been lately accustomed.

I will still only mention one circumstance related to the sick. We had among the number of those taken down with the fever a young man by the name of Bicknell of Barrington (in this state).[72] He was unwell at the time he came on board and had apparently the symptoms of the fever, and when we entered the [Providence] River, which was the 2nd day after leaving New York, in the morning, he appeared to be then dying but still retained his senses. He had heard from those around him that we were then in the river, and he requested to be assisted to be gotten on deck or as far as the hatchway, that he might once again view his native shore. He said he knew well his present condition and that death had already fixed his fatal, deadly arrow upon him, but he indulged himself with the hopes of a decent interment, and among his kindred and friends, [and] he spoke with the utmost composure and resignation. I was astonished at the change. He seemed to have all at once gained vigor and strength like a spark upon a dying candle which glimmers up at the moment it is to be extinguished.

72. Winchester Bicknell was born in Barrington, Rhode Island, on March 31, 1761. His father, Joshua, belonged to one of the old and prominent families of Barrington (*Representative Men*, 1025). According to a notice in the *Providence Gazette* (July 27, 1782), he died on July 20, 1782.

He pointed to the place where stood his father's house and which, he observed, contained all that was near and dear to him. We were then near the shore and the wind [was] very light. Our captain was particularly acquainted with his connections, which perhaps was his inducement to stop for this purpose, but we were all willing to abide by this occasionally short delay. He was assisted into the small boat [with] the two lads belonging to the sloop to row and myself in the stern sheets to assist him, for his strength began to leave him. While we were conveying him on shore to be buried with his ancestors, which in a feeble voice he said to me was his only desire and that God had heard his prayers, he lay his fainting head upon my shoulder and said "no more." As soon as we reached the shore, one of the lads was immediately dispatched to the house to inform his friends of our charge. They hastened down to the boat. They received their lost son and brother, but alas, they then received him a corpse.

> *[Among his friends his manly corpse doth] lie,*
> *[His] friends may shed a tear, when passing by.*
> [Freneau]

Arrival at Providence [and end of Captivity]

We regained the sloop as soon as possible after having delivered our charge and got immediately underway but did not reach up to Providence until the evening at 8 o'clock and anchored a small distance from the wharf of Messrs. Clark and Nightingale, a due precaution, as we had then several down with the yellow fever, but no quarantine laws or regulations were known among us in Providence. We were laid under no restrictions on account of the sickness or place we came from.

I recollect it was a fine, moonlit evening at the time we arrived, and our arrival was generally known throughout the town so that the wharf was filled with people, some from curiosity and some to inquire after their friends or kindred whom they expected were among us, and to all their questions a reply was made, and to some we had the sad and melancholy tidings to reply that their friend was dead and to others that they were left behind among the sick, and to some we had the pleasure to reply that they were on board and in good health, and to a few, "Your friend is on board but very sick." As soon as this sound reached the ear and it was ascertained that we had the yellow fever then among us, the wharf was deserted in a moment, not a person to be seen. The "old *Jersey* fever", as it was called at that time, was well known throughout the whole country and was known to be very fatal. Of course it was avoided like a pestilence by everyone.

We found the wharf deserted, and being very anxious to get on shore, as might be reasonably expected, we hauled alongside the wharf, and all that were well landed and disposed of themselves as they thought proper, and the sick were abandoned or left to themselves for that night, as no provision had been made for their accommodation or reception, and there was at that time no hospital in Providence or its vicinity. I was told, however, that some humane people had sent the sick some comfortable things during the night.

It was with great difficulty that the prisoners could get admittance into any house. The dread of the fever and their appearance operated much to their disadvantage, and the sick were absolutely refused admittance. It happened, however, that two of them had friends residing in town. One of them was Nathan Field, our cooper, and several had friends in the vicinity of Providence, and to such, notice was given early on the following day, who paid due attention by removing them immediately away, and the residue were comfortably provided for in the course of the next day by the responsibility of our owners, Messrs. Clark and Nightingale.

I do not recollect but one stranger among the sick. This was a young man, a mate of a ship from Philadelphia, who had assumed the name of one of our crew who was deceased and by that means got on board the cartel, as before stated, whose name I do not recollect. We, however, procured for him very good accommodations under the care of a humane and respectable lady (Miss Nelly Nixon), and Captain [then first officer] John Tillinghast and myself were then responsible for his support until his friends could be made acquainted of [his] situation, upon which subject they were duly informed, but death soon relieved us of our charge, as he survived only a few days after and was decently buried in the North Burial Ground in Providence.

> O'er [his tomb no] insulting Britons tread,
> Spurn at the [mound], and curse the rebel dead.
> [Freneau]

He had no money or effects of any kind, and his friends were made immediately acquainted with the whole circumstance, as related, and agreeable to his direction previous to his death. They wrote us in return in behalf of his widowed mother, thanking us kindly for the services and attention paid to her son and duly remitted the amount of our disbursements for their deceased friend and our late companion.

I have only now to say that when I commenced writing this my narrative, I had no idea that there would have been so many occurrences to mention, but having once entered upon the subject, I thought best to omit nothing that I deemed necessary to be related and have thus committed [them] to writing as they occurred to me while writing them, and if the remarks are not in due order, I have no one to apologize to [but myself], as the undertaking was purely to strengthen my memory which, thank God, is at this time very good, particularly to events which took place in my younger days.

Our crew, as I have before mentioned, was wholly composed of officers from Providence and its vicinity, and as companions I now recollect most of the officers, which it may not be improper here to mention, and although they are now numbered among the dead, they have many friends now living who well recollect everyone of them and a numerous posterity to bear their precious names in memory and whose duty it is for me to record. Although they did not all die on board the prison ship, yet all-devouring time has swept them all from the face of the earth, and the writer is the only one as an officer to relate the sad tale and rescue their names from total oblivion. Under this impression I have mentioned what death or memory can only obliterate.

The names of the officers of the privateer sloop *Chance of Providence* of twelve guns (and sixty-five men):

> Daniel Aborn of Pawtuxet, commander
>
> John Tillinghast of Providence, 1st lieutenant
>
> James Hawkins of Pawtuxet, 3rd lieutenant
>
> Sylvester Rhodes of Pawtuxet, sailing master
>
> Thomas Dring of Providence, master's mate (writer)
>
> Joseph Bowen of Providence, doctor
>
> Robert Carver of Providence, gunner
>
> Joseph Arnold of Providence, carpenter
>
> John W. Gladding of Providence, prize master[73]

73. For Daniel Aborn see note 12. For John Tillinghast see note 63. For Joseph Bowen see note 58. Sylvester Rhodes was born in Warwick, Rhode Island, on November 21, 1745. He married Mary Aborn, the younger sister of Daniel Aborn. Because he had served as an officer in the Rhode Island Regiment of the Continental army (and also was on Blackwell's Island when the cartel arrived), he was not allowed to be exchanged with his fellow privateersmen. In November 1782 he was finally paroled with the help of loyalist friends, but he died on the homeward-bound cartel on November 3 (Dandridge, *American Prisoners*, 432). Of the other officers listed here, as well as other crew members mentioned in the narrative, we have no further information except that most of the officers came from prominent Rhode Island families. It is clear that during the war, privateering was a socially acceptable, if not prestigious, way of life for Rhode Island's gentlemanly young men.

The narrative page for "The names of the officers of the privateer sloop *Chance of Providence*." (*Rhode Island Historical Society*)

[There were] several others as under officers whose names I do not now recollect, but of the whole crew of the Chance composed of about sixty-five men, the writer knows of only two (that is, the doctor, Joseph Bowen and James Pitcher) who are now living excepting himself, and in all probability, according to the course of nature, in a very short time even this scanty remnant will be among their number, and as relates to our enemies, I can only say [what] a poet has already said of them, which I recollect to have seen, and the observation is still on my memory,

> *Now cursed with life, a foe to man and God,*
> *Like Cain we drive you to the land of Nod.*
> *He with a brother's blood his hands did stain;*
> *One brother he, you Britons have a thousand slain.*[74]

"Ye sires, ye matrons, ye youth of America—remember the sufferings that [we] endured—indent them upon the rocks—cut them on trees—write them in indelible inks—and impress them on the minds of your offspring, that they may be remembered while our country bears the name of free" [Vandervoort, 67].

FINES

By the author (Thomas Dring), written at the early part of the year one thousand eight hundred and twenty-four, being the forty-second year after the transaction here related, yet such was the impression made upon the scene, and [with] continual thoughts of the transaction ever since, [that it] renders the whole familiar to recollection even as if it were an event of yesterday.

---

74. This poem is not by Freneau, nor does Dring claim it as his own. Dring's source for these lines remains unknown.

The narrative page for "Appendix to the Narrative." (*Rhode Island Historical Society*)

APPENDIX TO THE NARRATIVE

Recollecting that among Freneau's patriotic poems there was one upon the subject of the old *Jersey* prison ship, the description there given was so truly delineated that it made an impression upon my mind which could not be forgotten, and while [engaged] upon writing my narrative, this description of his would occur to my recollection and when suited, in my opinion, to the subject that I was then writing [on], I have occasionally introduced it into this work, that is, to the best of my recollection, and where the verse could not be wholly remembered, I have substituted a part of it and occasionally introduced some verses of my own composition to suit the subject I was then penning, or rather to suit my own fancy.[75]

I have also here made use of, in this narrative, some remarks or a description given in the oration delivered at the Wallabout upon the memorable occasion of the interment of the bones collected of those fallen victims and delivered by Benjamin De Witt upon this event. The picture is to the life, and every sentence ought to be handed down to posterity, but this not being my present object, [I] shall only notice a few lines in my narrative.[76]

But the great mass of this narrative was not only written by but witnessed by the author and is no fiction but [is] founded in facts under his own sad observation at the place of the scene, the old *Jersey*, and is one among the many events attending the revolutionary contest and not the least. The writer is very sensible that he cannot give due justice to the picture and has here related the principal occurrences without regard to order,

75. See note 9 and page xxxvi to the editor's introduction.

76. See note 4. It is curious that Dring chose to reveal that he had quoted from De Witt, but left previous Vandervoort and Fay quotations, as well as his source for all these quotations, unidentified.

knowing, however,. that the subject has met no exaggeration but in point of suffering falls in some instances short of the reality. It is recorded in a manner suited to the capacity of the writer and is the only subject upon which he ever attempted to offer a description of any kind.

I cannot drop the subject, however, without a few further remarks upon the final destiny of the old *Jersey* after the peace of 1783. At the expiration of the war, when the American remnant of prisoners was set at liberty or released from their confinement, the hulk was totally abandoned and then considered of no use, and the well known infection, which they knew adhered to her putrefied ribs, struck our former foes with dread. None was willing even to approach her, and she was abandoned entirely to the rats and the vermin within her putrefied bowels filled with pestilential air, and [she was] avoided as a pestilence by the passers by.

While the worms were doing their duty upon her disgraceful bottom, diligently at work as if conscious of the stain she had brought upon the British nation and even on common humanity itself, they soon accomplished this desirable event, and [with] the water flowing into her putrefied bowels, she sank at the Wallabout into her watery elements, and the eye was relieved from the sight of this disgusting object. Yet a part of her remains are yet to be seen at low tide, [which] leaves a testimony of the event, and with her descended names of some thousands of American martyrs who had cut their names upon her inside planks between decks, which if they had only been permitted to have them transcribed, would have filled a volume and given a clue as to the number who had visited those dark and dreadful abodes and [how] many paid the debt of nature.

Scarcely any prisoner ever omitted cutting his name. It seemed as [if] enrolling his name was a matter of exultation to him as being one of the victims who suffered and probably died in his country's cause. It is to be lamented that their precious names sank with the hulk, [which] buried them in oblivion, and all-devouring time has not left a trail behind of their numerous names, but their virtues shall not die with them.[77]

While writing upon the subject of the old *Jersey* in her present immersion, it brings to mind a present that I received from my friend, Captain Raymond Perry of the Navy.[78] It was a piece of the hulk about two inches square, which he had caused the workmen at the [Brooklyn] Navy Yard at the Wallabout to be taken from her remains, then observable after a lapse of more than thirty years. It was completely bored by the worms and resembled a piece of honey comb. Yet such part as remained was as sound as a rock and probably would continue so for a century to come. I have it still by me and shall endeavor to preserve it in keeping as a token of remembrance of my condition while confined within the ponderous planks of this once nauseous hulk of which this remnant constituted a

77. In an 1888 pamphlet titled *A Christmas Reminder* (for giving donations), the Society of Old Brooklynites published a list, taken from British records, of eight thousand names of *Jersey* prisoners. It must be incomplete, for the names of several known prisoners, including Dring, are not included (unless the listing "Thomas Dung" actually is Thomas Dring).

78. This would appear to be either Captain Christopher Raymond Perry (1761-1818), who late in life commanded the Boston Navy Yard and may have visited the Brooklyn Navy Yard, or his son, Captain Raymond H. J. Perry (1789–1826), who was assigned at New York off and on after 1820, and died nearby on Long Island. If Dring is correct that the donation was made about thirty years after his imprisonment (about 1812), and that the donor had died before 1824, the donor more likely is Christopher Raymond, who was also the father of two other famous naval officers, Oliver H. Perry (Battle of Lake Erie, 1813) and Matthew C. Perry (Treaty with Japan, 1854). See *Representative Men*, 483; Samuel Eliot Morison, *"Old Bruin": Commodore Matthew C. Perry, 1794–1858.* . . . (Boston: Little, Brown, 1967), 36; Calbraith B. Perry, *The Perrys of Rhode Island.* . . . (New York: Tobias A. Wright, 1913), 88.

part and from whose iron gratings I had passed anxious nights to inhale the passing breeze. I keep it labeled in commemoration of the event, and the donor is now numbered among the dead.

It is now more than forty years since her immersion took place, a space of time scarcely sufficient with the flowing tides to purify her bowels and destroy her vermin. But she is never more to rise upon the surface to distress the eye of the beholder, and although there is scarcely a vestige left, yet her polluted name will not be forgotten, for it is presumed that more men died on board this prison ship than anyone vessel that ever floated upon the ocean or anyone prison upon the face of the earth within the records of man in the same time.

[At this point Dring copied for eleven manuscript pages with only slight word variations (except for a few freely paraphrased segments) from the *Account* by Jacob Vandervoort. The subject matter (consisting of description and quoted documents, orations, etc.) includes collecting the bones of prisoners who had died and been buried at the Wallabout; the unsuccessful Tammany Society memorial to Congress requesting a tomb and monument for the remains, presented by Representative Samuel L. Mitchell of New York on February 10, 1803; the report of the Tammany Society Wallabout Committee dated February 1, 1808, calling for a fund-raising campaign to erect a tomb and monument on a donated piece of land near the Wallabout; a circular letter by the Wallabout Committee to the nation's newspaper editors dated February 11, 1808, requesting public financial support for the tomb and monument project; the cornerstone laying ceremony for the tomb (which was never completed) on April 13, 1808, including an oration by Joseph D. Fay; and the grand funeral procession and interment in a wooden vault on May 26, 1808, including a prayer by the Rev. Ralph

Williston and an oration by Dr. Benjamin De Witt. Dring has quoted and paraphrased frequently above from the *Account*, especially from the two orations. See note 4.]

I very much regret that I could not attend those funeral rites of my fellow sufferers whose bones I very probably assisted in laying under the bank at the Wallabout and which from time had been exposed to the eye of every beholder who passed by, but which had humanely been collected for a more suitable interment, which they so justly merited. Certainly they were the earthly remains of my fellow captives in misery and possibly my dear companions in life. My heart was filled with compassion and gratitude toward those who from pure principle of humanity, after the lapse of so many years, should put so noble and generous a deed in execution. Heaven reward them. They have the prayers of all the survivors of those unfortunate men who were among the sufferers and particularly of the writer, who was one of the number.[79]

The noble transaction just related brings to mind an observation made by one of the prisoners on board the *Jersey* while he was haranguing us on a Sabbath morning (and before relat-

79. Bones of prisoners hurriedly interred in 1782 on the Wallabout shore began to be exposed soon after the Revolutionary War ended. Caring people began to collect them and deposit them in an abandoned building dubbed the "Tomb of the Martyrs." In the late 1780s, the Tammany Society first petitioned Congress (unsuccessfully) for a fitting monument. A follow-up effort in 1807 also failed. In 1808, the Tammany Society conducted a ceremonial funeral procession, with speeches, from which Dring liberally inserted excerpts into his manuscript narrative. In 1873, the accumulated collection of bones was ceremoniously reinterred. In 1900, a new collection of bones emerged during excavation for an expansion of the Brooklyn Navy Yard. Finally, after decades of promises and planning, a Martyr's Monument was completed in Brooklyn's Fort Greene Park in 1908. See Burrows, *Forgotten Patriots*, 205–40.

ed in the former part of my narrative) when he told us that the time would probably be, or

"The day will come that shall to memory raise
"Piles on those shores to sound abroad your praise."

And thanks to God, his predictions have been verified, and I have been spared to see it accomplished [and] to record the events of that day. I am almost the only one now upon the face of the earth [among those] who were captured with me or who were my fellow captives at the time I have before alluded to, say one thousand seven hundred and eighty-two, being a lapse of forty-two years since the transaction of my sufferings on board the *Jersey* prison ship. The scene is fresh in my memory and never can be forgotten while I have the sense of recollection, and in order to strengthen my memory, I have committed [to writing] the whole transaction, well knowing that in a very short time there will be no one to relate the tale. They are simple facts, without exaggeration, founded in truth to the sorrowful remembrance of the writer, who witnessed the horrid scene upon the spot and partook freely of all the attending miseries.

INDEX

ACKNOWLEDGMENTS

The editor would like to thank the following for their substantial contributions toward publishing Thomas Dring's full prison-ship narrative with editing and interpretation of his experience in relation to Revolutionary War history and the history of warfare: The Rhode Island Historical Society and its then director Albert T. Klyberg for providing the opportunity in the early 1970s to transcribe, research, and edit the Dring manuscript narrative; the David Library of the American Revolution and its librarian Katherine Ludwig and historian Patrick Spero for encouragement and guidance in 2009 toward publishing the long-held edited manuscript narrative; Westholme Publishing and its publisher Bruce H. Franklin for believing in the value of publishing the Dring story and for valuable guidance through the publishing process; and Caroline Swain for editorial assistance and loving support.